Also by Da

Pulp Gospel – 31 bits of tt
Rebel Yell: 31 Psalms
The Bloke's Bible – Bits
The Bloke's Bible 2: The Road Trip – More bits retold
Sons of Thunder – A contemporary gospel
No More Heroes – Cain, Solomon & Jacob in a modern
tale of men, women, dads and crime

TOP STORIES

News Not History

31 Biblical Parables retold with humorous and serious comments

Index

Sowing the Seeds of Love
(The Sower)

Dave's Version

A rich businessman decided he wanted to give something to the people in his local village. Times were hard because of the austerity measures and he was keen to help folks out a bit. The problem was that the locals were a resourceful and self-sufficient people and they would be offended if he just rolled up on their doorsteps and gave them some money. So he brainstormed with his business manager and they came up with a scheme. Scratch cards. Free scratch cards distributed with the free local newspaper to every house in the village. Everyone could benefit, all they had to do was scratch off three boxes and see what they had won. The difference with these cards was that everyone would be a winner. There were no losers. There was no chance, whichever boxes you scratched off, that you would end up with nothing.

It would be a way of giving local folks some extra cash without it feeling too much like charity.

So he had the cards printed and inserted inside the week's paper.

Some of the scratch cards never made it to the houses. They fell out of the papers into the street and as it was raining they were washed down the drain or trampled in the gutters. Some of the cards arrived okay and were noticed by the readers but before the people could scratch off the boxes and see what they'd won the cards were mislaid, some falling down the back of the sofa others mistakenly thrown into the recycling. Other cards were spotted but disregarded by the readers as being too good to be true, and still others were found and scratched but then lost or forgotten about or eaten by the dog before they could be cashed in.

However some people did see the cards, read them, scratch them and take them to the local shop where they were able to cash them in and come home a lot richer. Some of those people won £5000, some £10,000 and some £15,000, but all of them were winners and benefited from the rich man's generosity.

The Bit Where Dave Explains How to Hear a Good Story...

A lot of stories have a hidden meaning, in the same way that a packet of cereal used to contain a free plastic zoo animal. Not everyone benefited though. Some people never got to the bottom of the packet and missed out on the bright yellow giraffe.

Others came across it totally by accident when lifting their spoon and finding a grinning hippo sitting on it. Some were so busy reading the back of the packet that they were chewing on a rubber crocodile before they knew what was going on. Some people read the news about the packet containing a free carnivore and were amused but reluctant to get too close, others were just annoyed by the dangerous possibility of swallowing a pink peacock.

It's easy to miss the plastic toy in the cereal packet of life. Reluctance, distraction, busyness, or not having a big enough spoon can mean we never find ourselves nursing the scarlet sabre-toothed tiger or the maroon woolly mammoth. But there are many chances. Buy a second packet and you may well discover the dirt-brown dingo you missed the first time round. Buy a third one and there could be a silver sloth waiting for you.

The man from Nazareth pointed out that to hear you must use your ears and to see you must use your eyes. Try it the other way round and you'll just be walking into walls and knocking your knee on every coffee table in the northern hemisphere. Some people like the truth on a plate, preferably spoon-fed. But like revenge, any dish served cold may not be too appealing. Better to have the truth served up in a tasty casserole with a choice of starter, the promise of pudding and a crusty bread roll.

Chewing on parables and allegories is not unlike eating paella. You have to pull things apart, take bits out, fiddle with the inedible bits and generally get your hands dirty. Don't expect cod and chips and a wodge of mushy peas here. The process can be quite exhausting - but worth the trouble. So keep your eyes peeled and your ears pinned back, your nostrils flared and your tongue on alert. You never know what you might find leaping out of the undergrowth when a story-teller strikes up...

Luke 8 vv 5-8

[5] 'A farmer went out to plant some seed. As he scattered it across his field, some seed fell on a footpath, where it was stepped on, and the birds came and ate it. [6] Other seed fell on shallow soil with underlying rock. This seed began to grow, but soon it withered and died for lack of moisture. [7] Other seed fell among thorns that shot up and choked out the tender blades. [8] Still other seed fell on fertile soil. This seed grew and produced a crop one hundred times as much as had been planted.' When Jesus had said this, he called out, 'Anyone who is willing to hear should listen and understand!'

The Serious Bit

I like this parable. It frees me up big time. Here's Jesus describing his work, and therefore the work of those following him, and it's all about sowing seeds, scattering little bits of hope all over the place, then leaving it to God and the different situations to see what grows. There's a subtlety to it – for some people hanging around on street corners with a sandwich board is the way to 'spread the gospel' but not for me. I'm about telling stories, doing little things, muddling through, trying to give people little moments of respect. All things I find in the way Jesus often operates.

You could call this the parable of the bad farmer. The guy goes out and indiscriminately chucks the seed all over the place. Surely a wise farmer plants carefully, in the best soil, with the best fertiliser etc. Not this man, not Jesus. He hurls bits of good news right, left and centre in the belief that, amongst the rocks and the road and the rubble there are patches of good soil, all willing to receive and bear different kinds of fruit. It's risky of course, the farmer may only get a small return on his work, but Jesus is confident that this way is worth it.

I like that.

?   ?   ?   ?

Rock Star Triumphs Over Swampy
(The Two House Builders)

Dave's Version

We're getting accustomed these days to floods and storms and our houses being overrun with bad weather, but last night's catastrophe really took the biscuit.

A motorhome on the edge of town was completely washed away. It started the evening not far from Townedge Swamp and ended the night fifteen miles downstream, flooded and upended in a ditch near Rocksville. The windows were torn out, the tires shredded and the body dented and skewed like an old coke can. What was all the more galling was that the van came to rest only feet away from a somewhat flimsier caravan. Somehow the older, smaller vehicle had survived that storm.

The owner of the caravan, Jack Star, explained how he'd anchored his home and his car – an ancient mini - using chains and giant bolts which he'd acquired from a nearby circus. Apparently he's a dab hand at reading the signs and could tell the storm was in the air, so he was taking no chances. He secured his mobile home to the biggest piece of rock he could find. Both his vehicles took a bashing but they survived the night intact and most importantly, were still in the place that he left them.

He was amazed to wake and see the huge motorhome upended nearby, a mere shadow of its former self, with the owner, Mick River, staring out at him through a shattered window. He was hanging upside down with, as Mr Star described him, 'his hair and his eyebrows looking like they'd sucked on a thousand volts'.

Jack took Mick in for a cup of tea and some R & R, lending him a phone to call the RAC. Mr River's motorhome is sadly beyond rescuing, but at least Mick himself escaped with his life, and his body intact. His sense of humour, however, was still missing without trace when we went to print.

'I told him that next time he should get himself some chains and an anchor,' Jack Star said, 'he hadn't done anything to secure that new wagon of his against the hurricane that hit town. He didn't thank me for the advice funnily enough. But if he doesn't take it it'll only happen again. And he'll lose another top truck.'

The Bit Where Dave Explains How to Build on a Swamp...

It's quite easy to build anything on dodgy ground. A garden shed, a tent, a medieval castle. The lads in Monty Python did it rather well when they were chasing the Holy Grail. The king built his castle on a swamp, and it sank. So he built another one. That sank. So he built another one. That burnt down, fell over and then sank. But the fourth one stayed up. Presumably because it was standing on the wreckage of the first three castles.

Probably best not to build a motorway on a swamp, but a bouncy castle, now that would work. Most of us build a few bits of our lives on swamps. Maybe a spare bedroom, the downstairs toilet and the kitchen. We have big bits of life nicely anchored to something solid, but there's nothing quite like playing fast and loose with one or two other bits.

You can build small chunks of your life on a swamp for a big chunk of time, or big chunks of your life on a swamp for a small chunk of time, but if you build big chunks of your life on a swamp for a big chunk of time you could sink without trace and be left in the long-term with little more than your dental records. It's not advisable.

The best people never go near a swamp. But as is often stated, the people who never fell in a swamp never achieved anything. You have to burn down, fall over and sink in a swamp to learn a few things. Even if it's only to find out who else is down there and which washing powder works best on the stains.

The easiest and most popular way to build on a swamp is by not listening to good advice. Things like 'don't stick your fingers in that socket', 'don't vote for the Monster Raving Loony party' and 'don't confuse toothpaste with superglue'. That sort of thing.

The man from Nazareth had just given out lots of wise advice and he finished it up with a story like this one, two homes, one of them surviving a storm, the other one burning down, falling over and sinking into a swamp. One thing's for sure, there's a storm on the way of one sort or another. Whether it's financial, emotional, weather-related, hormonal, gerbil-related or government ministerial-expenses-claim-related. Like death and taxes storms are a dead cert in life, the uncertain bit is whether we take any time to chain our caravan to the rock.

All kinds of rocks are available. Though some are made out of cardboard and string and were used in an early episode of Star Trek or Dr Who. These should never be relied upon to take your weight. Rock stars shouldn't be leaned on too heavily either. Many of them tend to fall over from the after effects of too many late nights, loud music and illegal substances. Movie stars are like rock stars, only different. They shouldn't be relied upon too much either. It's okay to read their advice in magazines, just so long as you laugh out loud and do the opposite of what they say. Someone with enough wedding rings for a football team may not be the Einstein of wedded bliss.

The storms of life are unrelenting, and without a rock and a chain, it's relatively easy to get upended in a ditch wondering where it all went wrong. You don't have to go to University to learn that. But it does help because there are many ditches in universities full of upended people. A college education can't protect you from the hurricanes of life. Especially when the weather men don't have a clue. And neither can the man from Nazareth, even though he does have a clue. In fact he laid a whole trail of clues. The storms will still come, like death and taxes, but getting enough of your life out of the swamp and onto a solid rock is something worth putting on your *to do* list.

Matthew 7 vv 24-27

[24] 'Anyone who listens to my teaching and obeys me is wise, like a person who builds a house on solid rock. [25] Though the rain comes in torrents and the floodwaters rise and the winds beat against that house, it won't collapse, because it is built on rock. [26] But anyone who hears my teaching and ignores it is foolish, like a person who builds a house on sand. [27] When the rains and floods come and the winds beat against that house, it will fall with a mighty crash.'

The Serious Bit

I build my life on all kinds of ground and some is more shaky than others. My lounge and kitchen maybe on a good slab of granite but you can bet that the bedroom could well be on the nearest available bit of soggy beach. At any one time I'm living with this contradiction. In fact, to become a Christian seems to me to embark upon a life of contradiction, believing in so many things that I cannot live out. Peace, justice, kindness, humility, truth. I do my best but the sand is never far from my door. I used to think that there was a very clear dividing line between the sand-castlers and the rock-merchants. The sandy guys were non-Christians, the rocky guys were the believers, the good guys, the ones who had it all sorted out. Of course, as life goes by and I meet more and more believers who are very far from having it all sorted out, I realise that it's one thing to believe in Jesus and who he is, it's quite another to build on what he said. Plus there are many people who do not call themselves Christians and yet are building on the words of Jesus.

It's worth noting that this parable is unusual in that it doesn't work on its own. It stands in the shadow of everything that Jesus has just described in what we now call 'the sermon on the mount'. Although, bearing in mind the number of jokes Jesus tells in that sermon, 'the stand-up on the mount' might be a better description. The parable about the two builders relates directly back to what he has just said about trouble, anger, lust, divorce, language, revenge, forgiveness, compassion, giving, praying, fasting, money, worry, criticising, persisting, and being fruitful or productive. So you could say that building on rock is not just about 'giving your life to Jesus' as much as taking note of his wisdom and following what he says.

Not easy.

?   ?   ?   ?

The Roman Candle
(The Light of the World)

Dave's Version

There's been an unprecedented rise in candle sales with the threat of power cuts in the air. Rising costs and increasing demand have combined to bring the days of a power shutdown ever closer. Memories of the mid-seventies are coming back to haunt those who lived through those candle-lit 'dark times'.

One man launched his own shocking protest last week. Josh Humble from Manchester put out his message on Facebook and Twitter, declaring that he was going to 'light up the world in a way no one could miss'. He said enough was enough, he couldn't conceal his frustration any longer he was going to write it large in the name of all those who are too poor to pay the extra costs. He said he was lighting up in public for those who had been left in the dark.

Only hours later he appeared in Trafalgar Square, doused himself in petrol and set himself on fire. The world was indeed watching. He was standing on the fourth plinth. Passers-by attempted to douse the flames but it was all to no avail. He'd done his job

too thoroughly. Josh died lighting up what he called 'the darkness of greed.'

He chose his day well – it was of course November 5th, and the biggest irony - Josh's maternal grandmother is from Italy, so he has Roman blood in him.

However, the story took an unexpected twist when three days later Josh was seen alive and well back in his home town of Manchester, riding a bus near the city centre. A friend on the bus spotted him, took a picture and within minutes it was all over Facebook. Josh slipped off the bus and into a crowd before she could follow him and he has since disappeared again. But friends of the 33-year-old insist the picture is clear enough for them to be sure. Josh Humble is back.

How he did the human candle trick is a mystery. Paramedics took the corpse away in a body bag, and he was placed in a London morgue. Police are refusing to comment, but no pictures of his body are available so the debate goes on. More pictures appear on Facebook with each day, some show him with clear scars from his ordeal, whilst others are quite obviously staged lookalikes. The pictures have gone viral, and extraordinary claims continue to come in of sightings all over the globe. From Teignmouth to Timbuktu.

Already plastic replicas of the flaming figure have appeared on the market, though many are claiming this to be a sick commercial enterprise. There have been calls for the banning of these models but sales on Amazon continue to rocket. The plastic Josh is now the second biggest seller behind the Amazon Kindle.

Who knows the truth? Will we ever? Did he fake his death for the protest? If so how? Stunt men use a technique known as a 'full body burn' for movies and television, wearing outfits coated in ice-cold fire-retardant gel before being set on fire. However, witnesses are adamant that Josh wore no protective clothing or face mask when last seen in Trafalgar Square. Unfortunately there are no pictures available of his appearance in the final minutes before the accident.

Conspiracy theorists claim the whole thing is merely a stunt staged by the IMF to distract from the continued global financial crisis. A feature in this week's Conspiracy Chronicle carried the headline: Melting Man Masks Monetary Meltdown.

And the sighting on the bus three days later, was that real? Or some kind of apparition? The friend, Magda Marilyn, has been interviewed several times by the authorities and is adamant she saw him. She claims too to have also received text messages and tweets.

Amongst all the hoo-ha and speculation one question hangs in the air. What was it all for? Will the people with the power take note, or will 'the darkness of greed' continue to put out the light?

The Bit Where Dave Explains How to Light Up Darkness...

There are plenty of ways these days to shed some light on a situation. One thing is certain though, you must never change a light bulb after dark. Remove a bulb from a socket in pitch black when you're not sure whether the power is on or off and you can be 100 per cent sure that the next thing you know your fingers will find out that the power was actually on. And your head will discover how hard the floor is.

These days you can buy tiny wind up torches so powerful they can be seen from the moon. Providing you can find them amongst the mess in your house, especially when it's after dark and the bulb in your lounge has blown again.

The solar-powered lamp may be out of the reach of the rich, most of us are too poor to light up our houses via some shiny panels in our garden, but the poor can sure afford it. Life in some African villages has been transformed by a single lamp which charges in the bright sunlight and lights up the dark for those who don't need a lot of light. We can't afford them because we'd need a solar lamp the size of your local Tesco to light up our houses, plus rainy wet summers with abandoned barbecues don't charge them up so well. Bank holidays in particular would be early-to-bed nights for everyone.

In the past we were told not to light our candles then hide them under a bushel.
There are four reasons why you shouldn't do that. Firstly because it would set the bushel on fire. Secondly because we don't own a bushel. Thirdly because we don't know what a bushel is. Fourthly it's a complete waste of wax.
According to the internet, which knows the absolute truth about absolutely everything, a bushel is a unit of dry volume equal to eight gallons. So you wouldn't put a candle under it, especially if it was 8 gallons of unleaded. Bushells (note the spelling difference there) is a selling and renting agency in London. They probably own and rent a lot of lights but they don't want to hide them under anything. They want you to rent and buy them.

There are all kinds of sources of light these days. Not just candles and burning bushels. There are spotlights, headlights, streetlights, smart phones, not-so-smart phones, absolutely stupid phones, pen torches, sparklers, cats eyes, red eyes in photos, fairy lights, goblin lights, Coke lights and Miller lites. Some lights are massive, capable of lighting up a sports stadium, others are just flickering glimmers. But they all bring light and chase darkness away. Any kind of light is extraordinarily athletic. It puts Michael Johnson in the shade. It travels at a speed of 186,282 miles per second. That's about the speed you reach when you realise you're late for work.

To sum up, lighting a light and then hiding it away is a daft idea, a waste of electricity, and no way to make a dark world brighter. If you have any kind of light, make good use of it. There is plenty of darkness out there, that's easy and cheap. Light might cost you something. But that's 'cause it's worth something.

Matthew 5 vv 14-16

¹⁴ 'You are the light of the world - like a city on a mountain, glowing in the night for all to see. ¹⁵ Don't hide your light under a basket! Instead, put it on a stand and let it shine for all. ¹⁶ In the same way, let your good deeds shine out for all to see, so that everyone will praise your heavenly Father.'

The Serious Bit

Much has been said about Jesus being the light for the world, so much so that it's very easy to forget that he also said, 'You are too.' You could think of yourself as a mirror. And mirrors reflect light without meaning to, or trying hard. Perhaps we all of us regularly reflect light and image, and we must choose what to stand near to to decide what we reflect. I vary my position a hundred times a day, often standing in the wrong place entirely and reflecting all kinds of dodgy things to the people I am near.

The second commandment is all about not making an image of God. This is because God already has an image. You. And a quadrillion others like you. Little mirrors, little chips off the divine block. And though we may ourselves often look in the mirror and dislike what we see and wish we could pay a lot of money to alter it, from God's perspective we all have great potential for reflecting his image to the world. Because his image is not so much about the right-shaped nose or chest size. It's about compassion and courage and justice and hope.

When Jesus was asked to name the second commandment he came at the image thing from another angle. He said, 'Love your neighbour as you love yourself.' That person nearby is the image of God too. That person is worth caring about. That person may well be the light of the world for us tomorrow. So by bringing light to them today we could be making an investment for the future.

Kerching!

? ? ? ?

Bad Smell Causes Riot
(The Salt of the Earth)

Dave's Version

An unnamed man was last night being held in custody helping police with their enquiries. He is charged with disturbing the peace and inciting public disorder. The man, who lives in Norbert Terrace, is accused of keeping a houseful of contaminated and rotting foodstuffs. He had been stockpiling degradable products for a long time. Neighbours had begun to notice the smell and the fact that he never put out any rubbish or recycling.

The food had started to stink. Badly. He had left it so long his cupboard was doing a good impression of a blocked toilet after a night in a curry house. Pretty soon the stench began to escape, seeping through the cracks in the walls and the gap under the door, and it then pervaded the kitchen like a bunch of invisible convicts who had dug a hole in their cell wall and snuck out through the prison sewer. Before long the whole house was overrun and the stench was oozing through the walls into the houses either side. The neighbourhood started to go downhill. Fast. Maggots appeared and multiplied like little tubular flesh-eating monsters. Cockroaches the size of rats and rats the size of dogs turned up from miles around and started eating their way through the walls and carpets. House prices dropped like a bomb and even the barge poles stayed away. One evening last week a mob surrounded 37 Norbert Terrace bearing torches and pitchforks. They were wearing gas masks and protective clothing. Windows were smashed and the door beaten down, which was probably unhelpful as a thick green cloud of putrid gas greeted the mob. Lice and flies poured into the street, along with a river of chemical waste. The angry crowd fought their way through the culinary carnage to find the owner cowering beneath a mountain of rotten cabbage and maggot-infested chicken innards.

The man was pulled from his vermin-infested house and all the furnishings hurled from smashed and open windows into the street. The frenzied crowd outside then destroyed and burnt everything. The fires burnt all night and could be seen three blocks away. The man lost everything.

The army was called out and the street immediately cordoned off. Three children and four old-aged pensioners are still lost somewhere amongst the degrading food supply. It's not clear why the man had stockpiled so much degradable food with such a short shelf life. Rumours abound that he had a pathological fear of tins, freezers, fridges and especially preservatives.

The Bit Where Dave Explains How to Preserve Things...

In years gone by salt wasn't so much for putting on your chips as for mixing in with things to make them last longer. This proved successful as not only did the foodstuff not break down, but it was also inedible. Especially for those at sea who were stuck with biscuits made of non-bio-degradable concrete and raw beef jammed so full of salt and maggots that there was very little room for any cow matter.

Salt is nature's can of Lynx. It keeps things publicly acceptable.

Ironically sweat contains salt but does not keep things publicly acceptable. On a hot day real Lynx is a whole lot more desirable than nature's prototype. However, a can of Lynx can only be relied upon to preserve trivial matters such as your place in the queue and girls swooning whenever they meet you.

It cannot be trusted to keep your marriage solid and your boss liking you. (Unless your boss is a group of swooning girls of course.)

Nature's own preservative is far more reliable for less sexy things like food. It's best not to spray Lynx on your sausages at a barbecue for example as you'll quickly lose friends and influence people... against you. In general salt stops things going off, and this will be very apparent if you put salt on your sausages instead of Lynx as your friends will usually then not go off.

People may wear Lynx but they'll still sweat salt, and if they want to improve their surroundings they need to rely more on sweat than Lynx. Salt for society is a different kind of salt altogether. A kind of metaphorical salt. And that's not Lynx. This kind of salt is a sweet smell for society but you can't get it in a black can.

Nowadays we have preservatives which were made to be added to everything to stop any kind of corrosion explosion. Preservatives aren't much to look at, you wouldn't put 'em in a dress and send 'em down a catwalk for the front page of the Sunday papers, but when they get working they do a unique job, they bring health and benefit, and magnify the flavour no end. In the past some snack foods have been too well-preserved. Unnaturally so. Like a TV celebrity who's had a few too many facelifts and not enough natural daylight.

People could be described as the preservative in the world. The salt of the earth. Which means they're not much good if you leave them in the packet or the salt shaker. They need to be randomly shaken up and shaken out and shaken in and shaken all about. Or, to put it the Lynx way, sprayed under the armpits of life.

Matthew 5 v 13

¹³ 'You are the salt of the earth. But what good is salt if it has lost its flavour? Can you make it useful again? It will be thrown out and trampled underfoot as worthless.'

The Serious Bit

Light and salt are often lumped together in the Biblical way of things. But whereas light is about finding your way and discovering where you are and where you are going, salt is more about wanting to stay where you are, making the vicinity more palatable, preserving it's goodness.

I used to think that this world was a bad place and heaven was the good place and the sooner we all shuffled off this mortal coil the better. We were all just hanging around, kicking our heels and waiting for Jesus to give us all jet-power to another life. Now I think differently. Why would Jesus want us to be salt unless we were supposed to improve our present surroundings?

So many of his parables are about living differently, rather than escaping this world for another one. That sounds to me like good news and bad news. Good news because this world is important and can be changed and celebrated and enjoyed and valued. Bad news because only heroes change the world. Only Superman and Spiderman and Batman. I'm not even amoeba-man. I'm the dirt on the bottom of amoeba-man's shoes. And that's on a good day.

But I'm discovering something. God knows what I'm like. And he's very used to making good use of people who feel as incapable as I do. It doesn't seem to phase him. In Biblical speak I'm a son of dust, and you are too, or a daughter of dust to cover all the bases for a moment. Only one person in the world is Superman, and that's only in a comic book. There are far more children of dust, and to mix the metaphor, he'd kind of like it if we morphed into salt from time to time.

?   ?   ?   ?

The Lost Car Keys
(The Lost Coin)

Dave's Version

Picture the scene – it's the day of the 100 meters final, you have tickets, you have transport, you have your mates waiting for you to get them there to witness the fastest man in history. You take your time getting ready, you want to look good, feel good, roll up in a cool, calm state of mind. The clock ticks on, you pace yourself. Somewhere down in the stadium the runners are getting ready to run the race of their lives. Only one of them will get it right, and you'll be there to see it. A story you'll tell forever. No feeling like it, being in that stadium tonight, looking down on that track, watching the fastest man in the universe.

Your phone goes, your mates are texting you, time to go, time to watch history being made. Easy does it. Check you have everything: iPhone, jacket, water bottle, keys... keys... keys... keys? Keys? Keys? KEYS!!!! Where the frappaccino are the keys? The car keys, the motor, the mean machine you're gonna roll up to your mate's house in, looking like Johnny Depp. They were there, right there. On the side. Waiting for you. Don't panic.

Stay calm. Don't break a sweat. Just look casually, check the obvious places. Nope. Okay. Check the unobvious places. Nope. Check the stupid places. Nope. Check anywhere. Check everywhere . Nope. Nothing else for it... it's hand-down-the-back-of-the-sofa time, check the worst places on earth. The sink, the plugs, under the toilet, down the toilet, check check check. Nothing cool about this now, sweat sweat sweat. Searching searching searching – never giving up. Got to find those keys. Nothing on earth is more important right now, nothing matters more. This is life and death. This is history. This is the only thing that matters now. Search search search, sweat sweat sweat. The ultimate cool is long gone now. But you're not stopping, you have to find those keys, have to get into that car and get to that stadium. Have to do it. Nothing can stop you. Don't give up. Never give up. Every ounce of energy, every last drop of sweat. The clock is ticking, the minutes are slipping away and you're going nowhere till those keys get found.

It's getting dark, it's getting late, but you will never give up, no matter how slim the chance, you are going to... wait! What's this? Hand right down deep, jammed down the back of that armchair, dog hairs, rotting fruit, soggy cheese, dead mice, live spiders, half a gluey pizza... There! What was that? Your fingers jab at some kind of cold metal spine... grab it and yank.. Go on – pull! Harder! There! A handful of stinking food and body parts - and there, right in the middle, shiny silver keys. A clump of them wrapped in matted hair and old finger nails. But you don't care about any of that. This is the prize. This is everything to you. This is the gold medal. This is the most beautiful thing on earth. Everything had been lost, till now. Now it's found. Now you know - the best thing in the world was worth looking for. It might as well have been a million pounds, or a diamond wristband, or a missing person. Worth every second, every bead of sweat. You went looking, and you found it. You're the victor. The man. Whoever wins that race in the stadium, you're the winner tonight.

The Bit Where Dave Explains How to Find Things...

Car keys are not easy to lose. Not at all. That's just a myth. Providing you have them in the ignition of your car you're fine. No problem. Mind you, the moment you take them out you're in trouble. I mean they could be anywhere then. In the nappy bin, in that pile of grass cuttings, down the back of the sofa, in the cistern, in the deceased hamsters shoebox coffin. It's best not to take them out of the car at all really.

The main thing to bear in mind when it comes to finding your lost keys is never to give up. You may become old and weak from lack of food in the process, you may grow a beard and miss your children growing up. But don't give up. Keep looking.

Of course it's not just car keys - life is strewn with mislayable things. House keys, your memory, the will to live.

Life is full of searching. It's a well known fact that at any given time half the population of England are involved in some kind of desperate rummage, whether it's for some keys, the TV remote, their partner, their children, their children's partner, the meaning of life, a way to get out of the washing up, a contact lens, or that odd sock that never makes it all the way from the washing machine to the underwear drawer.

Searching is a great metaphor of course. We often feel lost and need finding. Occasionally we find friends we thought we'd lost, and at other times we find friends we wish would get lost, but that's another matter.

If you lose a sheep the best thing is to call the police and describe it to them. Hairstyle and everything. But if you lose a sheep in a Bible story then the best thing is to keep looking for it as if it's a set of car keys. Mind you it's unlikely to be down the back of the sofa, or in your jacket pocket. The lost sheep is a metaphor for people who need finding. As is the lost coin.

When the coin/sheep/person is found then the next step is to throw a party. A big party. So loud you'll have to invite the police too, otherwise they'll be called out anyway to sort out the noise pollution. Now this party may cost more than the money you lost and have been hunting for all day, and it may involve killing and cooking the lost and found sheep. Which is why the story's not really good news for lost coins or lost sheep. It's really only good news for lost people who can then attend a massive public function thrown in their honour.

Luke 15 vv 8-10

[8] 'Suppose a woman has ten valuable silver coins and loses one. Won't she light a lamp and look in every corner of the house and sweep every nook and cranny until she finds it? [9] And when she finds it, she will call in her friends and neighbours to rejoice with her because she has found her lost coin. [10] In the same way, there is joy in the presence of God's angels when even one sinner repents.'

The Serious Bit

Jesus must have seen his mum lose coins; or his sisters; or the neighbours down the street. Either way he'd lived this story, as he had lived so many of the 'soap opera' kind of stories he tells. Jesus seems to tell at least three kinds of parables. Real life 'soap operas' like this one; folk tales about kings and servants and huge bags of money; and then history retold, in which he takes stories from his nation's past and rehashes them. The prodigal son is one of these, so too the rich fool. But more on that later.

What have you lost lately? I guess that any time you lose something, and let me warn you - it's gonna happen soon, it can serve as a reminder of the God of lost things. The God who comes looking, the God who won't give up, the God who throws wild parties. I need these kinds of stories and reminders, because, let's face it, God is invisible, and we can't really see him tearing his hair out because we're wandering off again. I don't know why he's invisible, it's one of those big questions. He is 'other', different, not of this world etc. But Jesus assures us that so many things in this life are flickering images, pale reflections of the God who is. So anyone searching for anything is a little YouTube clip of the caring creator. Someone hunting high and low, driven to distraction and refusing to give up, is a viral video of the dedication of God towards people who are regularly slipping down the side of the armchair of life.

It's heart-warming to notice that the outcome of this story is not, as we sometimes see in the supermarket, a clip round the ear and an embarrassing dressing down in front of everyone else in the queue – instead it's a ridiculous, wildly-out-of-proportion party. A party that may well have cost more than the lost coin. Like Babette, winning a fortune in the movie *Babette's Feast* and spending it all on a feast for a bunch of sour-faced undeserving villagers.

Party on.

?   ?   ?   ?

The Switch
(Jesus the Sacrifice)

Dave's Version

The last time I saw Jack Brando he didn't look like a winner. No way.
He picked at his finger nails the whole time as I questioned him. His iPod played on his knee as he stared into space, the tinny sound of hip hop spitting from the discarded earphones hanging by his left leg.

'Why did you do it, Jack?' I asked him. 'Why d'you throw it all away?'
Jack Brando had been the brightest light in a team of shockingly bright stars. One of the best teams to grace the games for years. Now the bright light was burning out, his eyes hard and cold, his toned body sitting on the bench with little energy, like a sack of discarded butcher's meat.

'We always said we'd stay clean,' I said. 'Compete properly. Why the drugs? You didn't need them. You got more talent in your left nostril than the rest of the field put together.'
The drugs ruined everything; the performance enhancing magic; the dead certainty of being the best. No chance of missing out on the gold and coming in second. That was for the rest of us.

The clean-cut, naturally-talented kid sold out just so he could be sure of glory. Shoot over the finishing line faster than a speeding bullet, faster than anyone else in that stadium. Faster than was possible. And the authorities could spot it a mile off. One tube of urine and it was all over.

He said nothing to me. Just stared into space as I questioned him. Then, as I stood up to go, he turned and said one thing, the last thing I ever expected. And I knew - I knew that he knew. I became the quiet one then, I just turned and walked away.

I'd known him all my life, most of it anyway, since we met at five, both of us snotty kids playing football in the playground with boys twice our size. We didn't care, we weren't scared, we'd take on the world and win. And we did. This week we'd proved it, two shining lights. No one could beat us. One of us on drugs the other on talent. No contest, we took on the world and won.

24

'Any explanation?' the coach asked as I passed him but I shook my head, there was nothing to say. This was devastating. One life ruined, another one made.
'Better get back to the stadium, they've waited long enough,' the coach said.
He spat on the sidewalk and hooked a dead cigar into the corner of his mouth. The guy was a dead ringer for Christian Bale, all he needed was a bat-suit and a black, pimped sports car and he'd be away. He wasn't much good at saving the world though, not today anyway. There was nothing he could do to make this better.

I got back to the stadium just in time, changed out of my jeans and stepped into the sunlight and the roar of the crowd. I waited by the track until the time was right and the names were called, then it was up on the podium, arms in the air and national anthem blasting out.

On paper it looked so unlikely, on the day it felt all wrong. But there I was. Gold medal winner. First over the line now that my best mate was banged up waiting his trial. With the winner out of the way I wasn't second anymore, no silver now. Just gold and glory. I tried to shrug off the guilt and the sick feeling in my guts but his face kept coming back into my mind, and those last words he said to me.
'I know Karl. I know.'

How had he done it? Why had he done it? What a loser, sticking himself on the line like that. Putting himself up for shame instead of glory, laying down his one chance of achievement and success, chucking that in the dustbin so that his best mate could step up onto the podium instead. There was surely a better way than this.

Afterwards, when the crowd had gone home and the coach was sitting there nursing his beer I wandered around the stadium again and stared at the place, quiet in the night and all cold now that the day's glory had faded.

Jack Brando hadn't looked like a winner when I last saw him. But then neither had I. One of us had crossed the line drug-assisted and it hadn't been him. One of us had crossed the line clean, and it hadn't been me. It was all wrong. And I don't know how he did it. Made the switch. Some miracle, some strange twist of fate, sleight of hand... a bizarre mystery. Either way I was free with gold round my neck, and it was all down to him.

The Bit Where Dave Explains How to Switch Things...

The man from Nazareth once said, 'the first will be last and the last will be first'. Which could be seen as confusing. A bit like saying the winners will be the losers, or the fat will be thin, or the short will be tall. Or the Terminator will be a Politician. Oh. Hang on. Well... that just goes to prove the strangest things *do* happen.

They don't tend to hand out gold medals for the slowest, shortest and least. So motivation is a tricky one here. Olympic events staged on these principals would last a long time, the 100 metre creep could take anything up to six months.

The man from Nazareth turned most things upside-down and inside-out. His message was a bit like your jeans when they come out of the dryer. You put them in all nice and tidy and they emerge the wrong colour, two sizes too small and with more twists and turns than an Agatha Christie mystery.

Agatha Christie would have warmed to the man from Nazareth, because just like so many of her characters he was not what he seemed. To all intents and purposes he was a poor builder from Nazareth. Whereas we know now he was a rich footballer from Luton. Okay he wasn't, but he was shockingly good at telling funny stories, going to parties and wittily second-guessing the politicians of his day. If they'd have invented *Have I Got News For You* in first century Galilee then Jesus would have been Paul Merton.

And no one expected that. When they met him it seemed as if he'd switched being religious for being a really great guy to have around.

Charles Dickens' classic book *A Tale of Two Cities* ends with a switch - one man giving up his hopes and dreams and freedom so that he can take the place of another. A bit like what happens when a new Prime Minster replaces an old one.

Jesus makes a switch like this but on an epic scale. More Peter Jackson than Charlie Dickens. A *Lord of the Rings* kind of switch.

He switches places with everyone, which is no mean achievement and not easily explained. Try thinking of a number too big to think of, or a colour that hasn't been invented yet. Or the Mona Lisa smiling. Or a politician apologising. It's the kind of thing that is just too hard to imagine. If you want to understand someone else then walk a mile in their shoes. That's what they say. I'm not sure it would help to walk a mile in Jessica Rabbit's stilettos though, you might never walk a mile again.

The man from Nazareth walked a mile in our shoes, then he went a second mile, and a third one.
He went so many miles no one could really keep up. And in the end it finished him off.
For three days anyway. Then he made another switch. He turned death on its head which confused everyone. Especially the Grim Reaper who had to let him go again.

Isaiah 53 v 6, John 1 v 29 & Hebrews 9 v 28

⁶ All of us have strayed away like sheep. We have left God's paths to follow our own. Yet the LORD laid on him the guilt and sins of us all.

²⁹ The next day John saw Jesus coming toward him and said, 'Look! There is the Lamb of God who takes away the sin of the world!'

²⁸ ...Christ died only once as a sacrifice to take away the sins of many people. He will come again but not to deal with our sins again. This time he will bring salvation to all those who are eagerly waiting for him.

The Serious Bit

I have to be honest, I don't understand how the crucifixion works. I used to wax lyrical about it quite easily and with a lot of flourish, but as the days have ticked by and the birthdays have stacked up like the ingredients in a Scooby Doo sandwich, I understand it less and less.

I know Jesus somehow took my place on that cross, but (to stick with the Scooby Doo analogy for a second) the mystery deepens for me. The plot thickens. To those first Christians Jesus's sacrifice came out of a centuries-old culture of sacrifice. They were well-used to the idea that you killed things in order to 'get right with God', lots of cultures did it. Some even killed their own children.

Quite early on Abraham discovered that God hates child-sacrifice. As he raised the knife to cut the life out of his own dearly-loved boy a voice from heaven broke in and shook him rigid. 'Cut that out! I don't want that!' Abraham came from a culture of child-sacrifice to the gods. This was news to him.

And yet here we are thousands of years later and God has to do the thing he hates. Child-sacrifice all over again. But now it's his own child, sacrificed in some strange way for the world. And for more than the world. I discovered recently that the original writing of the famous verse from John's gospel chapter 3 and verse 16: 'God so loved the world that he gave his only begotten son...' actually reads, 'God so loved the kosmos...' Kosmos means the way the world works, the systems of the world, the whole planet.

Two thoughts as I read that now. We instinctively interpret the word 'world' as meaning the people of the world, when it doesn't actually limit it to that. And secondly it says that God gave his son for the kosmos, he didn't just send him as a sacrifice for the kosmos, he sent him to live a life on this planet which included meals, laughter, teenage years, arguing, listening, lifting up the poor and the sick and the broken. Telling stories and jokes, going to parties and providing bread, fish and wine for crowds of people. And we are invited to believe in all of that; to follow the man who *was* all of that.

God so loved everything...

?   ?   ?   ?

Something Old, Something New
(New Cloth and New Wine)

Dave's Version

I went down to Nazareth the other day to interview the latest big thing. Putting Nazareth and big thing in the same sentence is of course odd. An oxymoron. I mean, nothing big ever came out of that two-bit place, now did it? Yet there I was, standing outside a humble carpenter's shop waiting to meet the new kid on the block. The cleaner came in at one point, scrabbling around in the dirt, scooping up the dust and the rubbish. It was only when he stood up that I realised it wasn't the cleaner. It was him. The next big thing. Mr Superstar. His face was wet with sweat and his hands were covered in grime but he still held them out to greet me. I didn't touch him. I didn't want to risk it. He just smiled.

Well, I panicked then and talked rubbish for a while, as you do when you're in the presence of greatness. It was the same when I met Tom Cruise and Prince William, I squandered half the time swooning and talking gibberish. I find I do gibberish very well on those occasions. The carpenter waited. He was very patient. He did 'waiting' very well. He looked off into the distance and narrowed his eyes, nodding occasionally and frowning sometimes as if the view in the back streets of Nazareth is one of those magic eye pictures you have to study hard to see clearly.

Eventually I gave him a chance to speak.
'It's been busy,' he said, 'I'm quite tired, I can't deny it, but time is short so I have to keep going. It's all happening so fast now, it's been bewildering for some - new experiences, new ideas, new relationships, new ways of acting and thinking. And that has created problems.'

He paused and massaged an old scar on his fist, a wound from his old days as a builder and carpenter.
Eventually he looked at me and went on, choosing his words carefully.
'You can't paint over a dark colour with a light one, can you,' he said, 'the old colour will show through, you need a new canvass. A new wall entirely. If you have four batteries in your radio and they are on the way out it's no use replacing just one. The old

ones will drain the life out of the new one, you need a whole new set. If you accidentally put diesel in a petrol engine, you need a new engine, it's not enough to top it up with unleaded and hope for the best. If you break your leg there's not much point just wearing baggier clothes to cover the damage. The leg needs proper care and attention. Major work. Any botched job, any lack of treatment will result in gangrene and then no amount of perfume will disguise the stink. I have old marks on my hands, fading scars, from an old life. But soon they will have new scars, new scars for a new kingdom. Chisel and knife wounds will be replaced by nail marks. It's the way. New scars for a new life.'

He paused and leant against the doorframe. He massaged the scar on his hand again. 'This is a new style of living,' he said, 'a new way of God working in this world. A way of forgiveness and compassion, justice and humility. You can't take a fistful of that and dust it over the top of the old ways of religion and philosophy. That would be like oil and water, bent on separation. This way of life is more like spices you mix into a dish and it permeates the whole thing, bringing new flavour and taste. Not so much sauce you spray on your food, but a new dish entirely. Full of goodness and nourishment.'

He flexed his fingers and sighed.
'People like the old ways don't they?' he said. 'In the past life was better. The music was sweeter, the weather was warmer, the prices were cheaper, the jokes were funnier. That may be so. But we are alive now, the new is here. The way of God has arrived. Do we want a part in it? Or do we want to hang on to what is past, what is distant, what is dying? It's not easy to move on, especially when others don't want to. I have lost family and friends myself, I know the distance that comes with misunderstanding, believe me. These are hard words I know, but I haven't come to bring a quick fix, I'm carrying a far reaching solution.'

The Bit Where Dave Explains About Old and New Stuff...

Some old things gain value whilst others lose it. And it's best to be very clear on this. No good taking your car along to trade it in for a newer one and expecting to get twice what you paid for it, although you will have to pay twice what the garage paid for your new one.

Many things depreciate the more you have of them. It's called the law of diminishing returns. Like cups of coffee or plates of doughnuts. Your first plateful of doughnuts tastes wonderful. Your second one not so good and by the third the taste has depreciated so much you're feeling extremely sick. This is also why Christmas gets less exciting the older you become. When you're five you've only had four other Christmases and you can't remember any of them so it's all new and shiny and full of the best presents ever - namely the cardboard boxes that things came in. By the time you're forty-five you've had forty-four previous Christmases and you know exactly how it works. And how much it costs, and who's cooking, and who'll be buying you socks again. And just about what time on Christmas day you'll start to lose the will to live.

Nostalgia is a pair of rose-coloured glasses. Or contact lenses if you're a little on the vain side. You view everything in the past as if it was better. You were thinner and smiled a lot more. Actually you don't need rose-coloured glasses for this, a photo album will do.

The problem with this is that you don't tend to take pictures of the bad times. In general you invite a professional photographer to weddings not funerals. Pulling out your iPhone and snapping away at the crem is not considered acceptable behaviour. So when you look back at your photos all you see are the days when the sun shone, the people partied and the children were... well children. We need more shots of the days when we're sitting on the sofa wondering where the next meal will come from. Or when we've eaten too much comfort food and we have our heads in a bucket. Flu and chicken pox could be caught on camera too. It would all keep things in perspective.

The man from Nazareth certainly had a lot of perspective. He knew that new things are a challenge if you like old things. Old time religion is not easily cast aside for new-fangled faith. In the same way that an old Teddy Bear with no ears and a loose leg does the job much better than a new one. Unless your dishwasher needs fixing in which case neither Teddy Bear will be up to the job. Old time religion is cosy and warm and friendly. New-fangled faith requires concentration and a willingness to listen, make mistakes, learn a bit, try again, make some more mistakes, learn and then make another mistake.

The past of course is a beautiful country where we didn't make any mistakes. Like Narnia or Middle-earth. The only problem with these places is that they don't exist. Walk into the back of any wardrobe and you'll end up with a broken nose.

The only constant thing in life is change. You could say that life is like a little boy who needs the loo - it doesn't stand still. The comforting thing is that people have always been wary of the new things. So that's nothing new, and we don't need to be wary of it. So even though people complain that the little boy never used to jig about like that, they're wrong, it's very likely that he did. Life has always been on the move. The man from Nazareth has always been on the move, the trick is keeping up.

Luke 5 vv 36-39

36 Then Jesus gave them this illustration: 'No one tears a piece of cloth from a new garment and uses it to patch an old garment. For then the new garment would be torn, and the patch wouldn't even match the old garment. 37 And no one puts new wine into old wineskins. The new wine would burst the old skins, spilling the wine and ruining the skins. 38 New wine must be put into new wineskins. 39 But no one who drinks the old wine seems to want the fresh and the new. "The old is better," they say.'

The Serious Bit

They say that the older you get, the less likely you are to change. You get more fixed in your ways. I see that in myself, at 20 I was up for many things, my life lay before me, anything was possible, very little was set in cement. And crucially I felt bullet-proof, that was a big part of it. At 20 I felt unbreakable, to coin the cliché – the world was my oyster. Even though I don't like seafood.

At 48 I feel much more breakable. Of course I'm still not old. Me? Me! Of course not. But I am aware of my weaknesses, aware of the ways life can go wrong and ambush you. I'm frayed at the edges now, creased and bruised in vulnerable places. It gets harder to believe in the miracles.

But Jesus encourages me to fight that, even with just a small ounce of energy. It's easy, and every year it gets easier, to look at the old days and think about how much better, how much rosier it was back then. In his autobiography *Dancing in the Moonlight,* Ronnie Barker recalls lying in a moonlit field with a girl he loved, watching her dance under a warm moon. He realises how fleeting and precious were his youthful days and he says this: 'It was a silver time. I too was dancing in the moonlight.'

I read that ten years ago and it still tugs at my nostalgic heartstrings. Perhaps now more than ever, I want the old days back again, I want to be young. And Jesus knows that. In this particular case, in the parables about old and new wine, he is calling his contemporaries to see the new thing he is doing for the kingdom of God and the kingdoms of the world. He is bringing one into the other and if they try and hold onto the old days when life seemed easier and sweeter then they will miss this great new thing. God doesn't stand still. Yes, he's reliable, yes his trustworthy character is the same yesterday, today and forever. But that doesn't make him old-fashioned, he moves with the times, he works with the new generation. He communicates with the language of today.

Let's not miss that.

? ? ? ?

Aldemia Goes to War
(Building a Tower and Planning a War)

Dave's Version

The world rocked last night to the news that the tiny state of Aldemia has declared war on Great Britain. Aldemia, a small island country off the coast of Africa has no army, navy or air force and never has had one. The British government is fairly sure it has no weapons of mass destruction – though it has been wrong on this issue before.

Aldemia claims it is tired of being labelled as 'that tiny island state off the coast of Africa' and is ready to settle the score with Britain. How they intend to do this is as yet unclear, unless they are going to swim 845 234 miles across the Mediterranean Sea one man at a time, and then attack London in their trunks, snorkels and swimming goggles. Aldemia possesses no submarines, ships or aircraft carriers. It's even rumoured to be short of bicycles.

Never has a country of so few declared war on a country of so many with so little chance of even meeting the enemy. It all seems over before the battle has begun. Politicians are at a loss to understand what can be gained by so much rhetoric. There is little threat of a bombing campaign by air or by post unless they intend to blitz the country with computer viruses via email. Franklin D Roosevelt once said, 'We have nothing to fear but fear itself.' In this case we don't even have that. There really is nothing to fear. Frankly, the situation is baffling. Why declare war when you have no chance of even firing the first shot, never mind winning?

In a gesture of goodwill the government declared last night that it is now politically incorrect to refer to that tiny island state off the coast of Africa as 'that tiny island state off the coast of Africa'. So, one victory for that tiny island state anyway.

In other news here at home London has declared that it is to build a second Millennium Dome, even thought the first one was a major disaster. How quickly the past has been forgotten and history rewritten. The new committee is certain they can make this new building more impressive and more lucrative than the last.

It is not yet clear where the funds will come from to finance the project as Britain really is now strapped for cash, and no one is holding their breath to see how soon it will be completed. Yet again there seems to be little idea about what will actually go in the new Dome and what its purpose will be. Apparently Simon Cowell has offered to host a TV programme where the public would have the chance to offer their ideas and suggestions. It would be called The Dome's Got Content.

The Bit Where Dave Explains How to Dream Big Dreams...

History is littered with non-starters. Good ideas we once had that never got off the page, or off the ground, or off the back of our hands, or out of our heads. The rubber hammer - that was a non-starter. Along with the paper car and the chocolate tea pot. And the over-80's World Wrestling Foundation.

Some bad ideas do actually make it into real life. The cabbage soup diet. Mr Blobby. Hip hop. Pierce Brosnan singing. These are ideas that we know deep down should have been non-starters, yet somehow they made it off the page and into our lives.

We plan many things, and some people make a career out of planning things. Shopping lists, 'to do' lists and 'not to do' lists litter our lives like the inserts that fall from the Radio Times. It's easier to plan things than to actually do them, and talking big is much better than living big. Living big involves hard work and careful planning and commitment, where as talking big just requires a mouth. And an audience.

We all like to dream big dreams, to while away the boring moments of our lives by imagining a better but absolutely impossible world. A sort of totally impractical alternate reality.
Politicians like to do this, they call these daydreams manifestos. Most of us do it on the quiet but politicians do it on the TV.

An old proverb states that 'If wishes were horses beggars would ride.' But a lesser known proverb states that 'most wishes just refuse to have riding lessons.'

The man from Nazareth knows what it is to be realistic. 'It's no good', he says, 'promising to go riding across the African plains tomorrow if you have no plans to put down a deposit on a horse.'

Difficult things need thinking through. You can't climb Everest in an armchair. Though you would make the Ten o'clock news. You can plan a lot of things in an armchair but you can't actually do them. And if you plan to be a disciple then there's no point complaining when you find yourself in a difficult place, miles away from your daydreams and 'to do' lists.

Being a disciple is very different to being a daydreamer. One requires blood, sweat and tears, the other requires a lilo, sun-cream and a swimming pool. I'll leave you to discern which is which.

Luke 14 vv 28-33

28 'But don't begin until you count the cost. For who would begin construction of a building without first getting estimates and then checking to see if there is enough money to pay the bills?

29 Otherwise, you might complete only the foundation before running out of funds. And then how everyone would laugh at you! 30They would say, "there's the person who started that building and ran out of money before it was finished!"

31 'Or what king would ever dream of going to war without first sitting down with his counsellors and discussing whether his army of ten thousand is strong enough to defeat the twenty thousand soldiers who are marching against him? 32 If he is not able, then while the enemy is still far away, he will send a delegation to discuss terms of peace. 33So no one can become my disciple without giving up everything for me.'

The Serious Bit

When Jesus talked about buildings and construction work he had a particular place in mind. Herod was rebuilding the Jewish temple, and not just the temple, but a complex of buildings that would be something akin to a first century Disneyland. When he was 12 Jesus went on a pilgrimage to the temple and was so caught up with the place he didn't want to leave. He loved bantering and swapping stories with the religious leaders there. It must have been an extraordinary experience for an impressionable teenager. But Jesus is not impressionable now. He sees through the façade. Building a magnificent temple is one thing, but choosing to side with God and all he stands for, now that's an entirely different proposition. Not unlike going to war, and you don't do that unless you are prepared. Or think that the enemy might just possibly, maybe, perhaps have weapons of mass destruction.

The invasion of Iraq and the great chemical weapon hunt serve as a good parable here. 'Nobody invades a country in order to confiscate their WMD's,' Jesus might say, 'unless they've done their homework and know that the weapons are actually there.'
Ouch!
And some folks might laugh and nod and get the joke and appreciate the point, and others might flinch and recoil and be blooming annoyed because they think it was a good idea to invade Iraq anyway. Others might wonder why Jesus is bothering to comment on a political situation when he should be talking about religion.
And those are the kind of reactions Jesus would have received to his parable about construction work. The temple was right there, in your face, it was pretty obvious, and there were mixed feelings about Herod and his plan to rebuild it.

I've been to many meetings where invitations have been given for people to give their lives to Jesus. I don't think I have ever heard someone say, 'Look. It's a really important thing and a tough decision to make. I don't want to rush you. So go home, think carefully about Jesus, make sure you know what he's offering and then decide if you want to follow him.'

Risky that.

?   ?   ?   ?

Bank Manager Goes Money Mad!
(The Unforgiving Servant)

Dave's Version

A bank manager has been accused of insanity over a recent decision regarding one of his customers.

The woman came to see the bank manager one day and, according to eye witnesses at the bank, the remarkable conversation went something like this:

'Ah! It's you!' said the manager, 'I've been expecting you. It's Mrs er... what's your name again?'

'Broke,' said the woman.

'I know you are,' said the manager. 'But what's your name?'

'Broke,' she said with a sigh. 'I'm broke. And I'm Mrs Broke.'

'Ah,' said the Manager. 'I see. Now then Mrs Broke. It looks like you owe us a lot of money.'

'Yep.'

'A huge amount of money.'

'Yep.'

'An obscene amount of money.'

'Yep.'.

'Thousands and thousands and thousands.'

'Yep.'

'So,' said the manager, 'how much have you got?'

'Er... Ten pounds fifty,' said the woman.

'Hmm... Ten pounds fifty. That won't buy me a new cigar. Looks like we'll have to have your house back then.'

'Please – no!!' screamed the woman. 'I have fifteen children, and a dog and a cat and four guinea pigs and a hamster and fifteen rabbits. Please don't throw us onto the streets. We have nowhere else to go.'

'Yes, but what about this mortgage? It must be paid. And the present financial climate is not in your favour is it?'

'No it isn't. But I can't pay it back.'

'Then we have to take your house.'

Mrs Broke fell on her knees pleading. 'No. No. No. NOOOOO!!!! Please, please, please, please, please...'

The bank manager however, was a compassionate man.

'I'm a compassionate man,' he said, 'so I'll tell you what I'll do. You can't buy the house – so I will.'

Mrs Broke tried to stop him. 'No! Please...'

'And,' he said, holding up a hand to silence her complaints. 'I will give it to you. Forever.'

'Oh that is so unfair, how dare you... I mean... I'm just a... hang on - what did you say?'

'I'm giving you the house. Forever. It's yours. No debts. No repayments. No rent.'

'You're kidding? No debts? No repayment? No rent?'

'That's what I said.'

'No debts? No repayment? No rent?'

'Absolutely.'

Mrs Broke threw herself on the floor and wrapped herself round the manager's ankles. 'Thank you, thank you, thank you, thank you. Tell you what – our guinea pigs are pregnant – you could have one of the babies if you want.'

'Er… thanks – but no thanks. Bye.'

The manger made attempts to leave but the woman had him by the leg and was refusing to let go.

'Er… I have to go now,' said the manager.

She hung on.

'Bye then,' he said, shaking his leg violently.

It took a while but eventually he shook her off, forced a smile and left. Mrs Broke stared after him for a while and was still in a daze three minutes later when she wandered out of the bank and a friend of hers went past.

'Hey Sally,' Mrs Broke said, when she saw her friend, 'guess what! I just got my house back – the bank manager bought it for me. The debt's cancelled.'

Sally was amazed. 'Wow!' she said. 'That's brilliant. Can I meet your bank manager?'

'Yea, whatever,' said Mrs Broke. 'So anyway, remember those deck chairs I leant you for the garden. I need them back now.'

'What do you mean?' asked Sally.

'Those chairs,' said Mrs Broke, 'I need them for my house.'

'I don't have them,' said Sally, 'I was broke so I sold them at a car boot sale. I got a good price.'

'Where's the money then?'

'I'm sorry I really needed it for food shopping.'

'Food shopping? That was my money!' screamed Mrs Broke. 'How dare you sell those chairs and spend it on yourself. I want it back. You pay me every penny by next week or I'll come round and take something of yours.'

Just then the bank manager went past. He smiled when he saw Mrs Broke, though he didn't come too close in case she grabbed his legs again.

'Ah, Mrs Broke,' he said, 'this a friend of yours?'

'She was,' Mrs Broke said, 'Not any more. She took what's mine and won't give it back.'

'I can't afford to,' said Sally.

'Maybe you should let her off?' said the manager.

'What?' said Mrs Broke. 'Why? She owes me.'

The manager smiled again. 'Didn't anyone ever cancel your debts?' he asked, and he strolled off.

The Bit Where Dave Explains How to Miss the Point...

It is very easy to miss things. Like buses and archery targets and the girl you fell in love with when you were six. And some things are worth missing. Like the French Revolution for example. Great to read about, not so much fun if you're horizontal and there's a guillotine blade looking down at you glinting in the French sunshine. Me playing football is well worth missing. So is William Shatner singing *Rocket Man* at the 1978 science fiction awards. Although this is one of those things that is so missable you really shouldn't miss it.

Many people missed the man from Nazareth when he died - but only for three days. After that you couldn't miss him. He was everywhere. Till he went away again, then people really did miss him. Until the Roman Empire made it illegal to miss him and people died over the issue. Nero was a particular fan of encouraging Christians to forget. He lit the kind of fires that would never go out - Christians. Until another Roman Emperor came along and made it illegal to light those kinds of fires and made it highly legal to be a Christian. Then the whole Roman world got converted overnight.

Organised believing is okay but it kind of misses the point really. The man from Nazareth liked people to choose. Choose to follow or not. Choose to forgive or not. Choose to be generous or not. Organised believing is like having a kind of heart-bypass operation. You don't have to do any choosing or soul-searching you just have to tick the right box on the form whenever they decide to count the population. You can of course do it all online now too. You don't even need a pen. So it's easier than ever to have that heart-bypass and be a tick-box believer.

Do be careful who you sign up with for other kinds of heart-bypass procedures though, there are all kinds of backstreet surgeons at work these days and you don't want to have your body parts hacked about with a chisel and a Stanley knife by someone claiming to be qualified, who none-the-less works by the light of a local tattoo shop. Likewise be cautious who you listen to re the soul-searching, a man dressed like a cowboy who got ordained on a website and claims to be the next son of God is unlikely to have access to the Almighty. Best to put him on hold and search for other kinds of help.

You can get plenty of help if you would like to miss the point. Filling your life with things out of a catalogue that fell out of the *Sunday Times* means you can keep yourself distracted with vital choices like what colour your new 3 piece plastic Chicken Jazz Band should be or how many Meerkat Garden Wobblers you might need at any given time. Talking about the weather is a fine distraction I find, and worrying about things you have no power over. The end of the world for example and whether you turned off the tap and locked the back door when you're already sitting aboard that plane to Australia.

The important thing about missing the point is to be totally focussed on the minor details, or the wrong details entirely. If your life has been made better then the chances are you could actually make someone else's life better. But not if you're going to miss the point. To truly miss the point you must just make everyone else's life worse. For example, if you've just been let off a very big hook by someone benign then make sure you hang someone else on that hook.

Matthew 18 vv 23-35

23 'For this reason, the Kingdom of Heaven can be compared to a king who decided to bring his accounts up to date with servants who had borrowed money from him. 24 In the process, one of his debtors was brought in who owed him millions of dollars. 25 He couldn't pay, so the king ordered that he, his wife, his children, and everything he had be sold to pay the debt. 26 But the man fell down before the king and begged him, 'Oh, sir, be patient with me, and I will pay it all.' 27 Then the king was filled with pity for him, and he released him and forgave his debt.

28 'But when the man left the king, he went to a fellow servant who owed him a few thousand dollars. He grabbed him by the throat and demanded instant payment.

29 His fellow servant fell down before him and begged for a little more time. 'Be patient and I will pay it,' he pleaded.

30 But his creditor wouldn't wait. He had the man arrested and jailed until the debt could be paid in full.

31 When some of the other servants saw this, they were very upset. They went to the king and told him what had happened.

> ³² Then the king called in the man he had forgiven and said, 'You
> evil servant! I forgave you that tremendous debt because you
> pleaded with me. ³³ Shouldn't you have mercy on your fellow
> servant, just as I had mercy on you?' ³⁴ Then the angry king sent
> the man to prison until he had paid every penny.
> ³⁵ 'That's what my heavenly Father will do to you if you refuse to
> forgive your brothers and sisters in your heart.'

The Serious Bit

Forgiveness is powerful currency. We love to withhold it when
revenge is in the air. Being too forgiving too quick can make us
look terribly weak and naïve. Some people manage to get
through their whole lives without doing too much of it. Especially
men, and boy can they get chewed up. I once heard a
memorable little quote about harbouring bitterness towards
someone.
It's like drinking poison yourself and expecting your enemy to die.

There's just something so tasty about the idea of getting your own
back. In the movie *Gran Torino* Clint Eastwood's character Walt is
chewed up inside about the things he saw and did in Korea. The
local priest knows this and begs him to come to confession. Walt
refuses so the priest says to him, 'I know nothing about war, but I
have seen a lot of men who have confessed their sins, admitted
their guilt and left their burdens behind them.'

In this parable Jesus paints a picture of what will happen when
you know you've left your burden behind. You become more
forgiving towards others. Or at least, that's the idea. It's not
necessarily about feeling more forgiven, though that's a good
outcome. Primarily when my burden is lifted, I should then go out of
my way to lift burdens off others. Not place more onto them and
make their lives worse. This is the fruit of forgiveness, more people
get forgiven.

More people become 'light' hearted.

?   ?   ?   ?

The Lost iPod Song
(The Lost Sheep)

Dave's Version

I heard recently about a guy who kept all his music on his iPod. This was really good news because it meant he had it all in one portable place. It was really bad news because it meant he had it all in one portable place – and that meant there were 40,000 songs on it. One day he heard a song on the radio. An old song he loved. It was called *Never Give Up On a Lost Soul* by Funky and the Children. At least that's what he thought it was called. It was an old song he had once put on his iPod and forgotten all about. A song he grew up with, a song he used to play when he was in love with Fatima in year six at school. It brought back long lost memories of his childhood.

So he thought he'd find the track again. He grabbed the music machine and started flicking through it. He knew he had it on there, it was just a case of tracking it down. Wouldn't be difficult. Just a minute or two and he'd have it. Ah! No, not there, strange. At least, it wasn't there under that title. He tried a few alternative titles. If it wasn't *Never Give Up On a Lost Soul* maybe it *was Never Give Up On a Lost*

Soldier. Nope. How about *Never Give Up On a Lost Son.* Nope. *Never Give Up On a Lost Sausage* ? Still no joy so he tried searching under the artist. No, not under that name either. Unless that wasn't the right artist. So he tried a few alternatives. Monkey and the Chickens? Chunky and the Mittens? Hunky and the Kittens? Manky? Minky? Nope.

His friends came round to see if he wanted to go out for the evening. He couldn't, he had to find this song.
'Look it up on YouTube,' one of them said.
'Yea, or Spotify,' said another. He refused.
'I've got it on CD,' said his sister.
'I've got it on vinyl,' said his mum.
'I've got it on an old 78,' said his dad, who was probably lying.
But he wouldn't listen. He knew the song was somewhere on his iPod and he was intent on tracking it down. His friends left. His girlfriend phoned up.
'I've got a surprise for you,' she said.
'What's that ' he asked, still flicking through his songs.
'I've got two tickets to see Funky and the Children!

Tonight!' she yelled down the phone. 'Remember them?'
'Course I remember them I'm trying to find one of their songs right now.'
'Well don't worry, they'll probably play it live for you if you come to the gig with me.'
'I can't.'
'What!'
'I can't, I've got to find the song. I'm sure it's on my iPod.'
'This is ridiculous!' she said.
'Come and hear them. They're only in town one night.'
'I can't I bought this track and it's mine. I want to find it.'
'You're mad.'
'Maybe but I know it's here.'
She hung up. He went on searching. The hours ticked by. Everyone else went to bed. More hours ticked by. The phone rang again.

'It's me,' said his girlfriend. 'The concert was brilliant. And they did your favourite song.'
'Which one was that?' he asked.
'You know, that one you always loved. *Perseverance Pays Off.*'
'Which one's that?'
'You know – the one you always thought was called *Never Give Up On a Lost Soul...* That was the second line of the chorus, the first was the title - *Perseverance Pays Off.*'
'No it's not,' he said, 'it's not called that.'
'Look,' she sighed, 'we've had this argument ninety-nine times, I'm not having it again. Don't believe me – look it up on your iPod.'
And she hung up.
He did look it up.
End of story.

The Bit Where Dave Explains the Art of Crowd Following...

Peer pressure is a wonderful thing. It keeps organisations very well organised - like schools and churches and bus queues. As long as everyone follows the crowd the system works like clockwork. If anyone bucks the trend then you're in trouble. Martin Luther nailing his own wild ideas to the church door caused an awful rumpus. Thomas Cranfield changed education forever with his crazy notion that all kids, poor and rich, deserved an education. *High School Musical* didn't change education much at all, though many kids did try to sing and dance whilst playing bastketball for a while.

Giving in to peer pressure makes you do silly things, like wearing masks. I don't mean rubber Ronald Reagan headgear that criminals use to rob banks, I mean the kind of masks that cover up who we really are and make us look much better than it's possibly human to really be. Nobody wants people running around showing their true selves so these masks are popular. Fortunately they're also free otherwise we'd all be bankrupt. Or should I say - more bankrupt.

Not giving in to peer pressure makes you do even sillier things, like showing your true self. Being up front about your failings and weaknesses. And chasing after lost sheep.
Fortunately the man from Nazareth did not give into peer pressure so he was quite happy to chase after lost sheep and look silly. 'Call off the search' were four words that didn't feature much in his vocabulary.

He may have appeared a little crazy at times but then to change things you often have to look mad. Mind you, there are different kinds of madness. Running around with your pants on your head will not achieve that much. But burying your pants in the garden, that's another matter altogether. The Old Testament prophet Jeremiah pioneered the whole idea of rotten undies as a metaphor for rotten people. It still hasn't yet caught on properly, though many boys do display a lot of rotten underwear these days, when they can't afford jeans that will fit them properly.

At the end of the day you'll know you're following the crowd if moving forward is easy. If you keep banging into other people and getting your shins kicked you may well be going against the grain. Or just playing rugby.

Matthew 18 vv 12-14, Luke 15 vv 1-10

12 If a shepherd has one hundred sheep, and one wanders away and is lost, what will he do? Won't he leave the ninety-nine others and go out into the hills to search for the lost one? 13 And if he finds it, he will surely rejoice over it more than over the ninety-nine that didn't wander away! 14 In the same way, it is not my heavenly Father's will that even one of these little ones should perish.

The Serious Bit

Another searching story. Jesus liked them so much he told three of them. In Luke's version of events he tells all three in a row.

Blam! Blam! Blam! Three barrels hitting that point home. Two of his stories are soap opera events, one is history retold.

Now my guess is that you haven't lost a sheep lately, though knowing my luck you're probably a farmer who has just this minute come in covered in muck and thorns... but I think you get the point. When Jesus told stories about lost sheep they were symbolic and vital. The Jewish faith was chock full of images of shepherds and sheep. And many of the people listening were subsistence farmers who may well have owned a sheep. They lived this story from time to time and they got the joke. Been there, done that, got the lost sheep to prove it.

In the Old Testament when the prophet Nathan wanted to convict the wayward King David he used a parable about a sheep, but this one wasn't lost, it was stolen. And then roasted. The people of Jesus's day knew that story. The prophet Ezekiel had described shepherds as being bad leaders who gorged themselves on the defenceless flock. Now here comes Jesus with a very different tale. His sheep are people who have done a runner, found a hole in the fence and scarpered, and now here comes a good shepherd, not afraid to get his hands and his clothes dirty, diving into the dark places to bring off the rescue attempt. This shepherd does not have a halo and a bright white nightie, this shepherd gets down and dirty with his sheep; he wouldn't be much good if he just wanted to stand around with gelled hair and a shiny crook, looking good.

I have heard different stories regarding the 99 sheep left behind. Some say a shepherd would never do that so this makes the story a joke and the audience would laugh at this. Others say leaving 99 untended makes the shepherd a bad one. So now we've had a bad farmer sowing seeds all over the place and a bad shepherd who risks losing 99 sheep just to find one. Jesus is not looking good is he? Or maybe – he's not worried about looking good. He's come for the people that others often disregard and overlook. In another parable, about workers getting hired, the hero bothers to hire those who, at the end of the day, have not been chosen by anyone else. More lost sheep then. Overlooked and disregarded.

The bad shepherd/bad farmer clearly has a very different agenda.

?　　　?　　　?　　　?

The Street Party
(The Great Banquet)

Dave's Version

Recently I met a woman who threw a big party. She had lots to celebrate, she had just passed her driving test and finished her Open University degree and that weekend she won a thousand pounds on the lottery. So she decided to spend it all on her friends. She bought food and drinks and she decorated her house and she sent out lots of invitations via Facebook and Twitter. She had loads of friends so she knew she would need to organise plenty to eat and drink for them.

No one came. Instead the text messages began to trickle back in.
Sorry I'm going away next week, I need to pack.
Sorry, I'm already busy. Got another party to go to.
Sorry. I'm getting my hair dyed.
Oh, I've had a busy week.
Oh, I've had a busy day.
Oh, I'm watching the X Factor Final.

She sat on the stairs and cried. This was one of the best times of her life, and nobody cared.

She was desperate to celebrate and her friends wouldn't come. She'd grown up with some of them too, known them all her life. She grabbed her coat and went for a walk, she had to get out of that house. That empty party house. She found herself walking through town, and came across a massive queue outside one of the town centre churches.
'What's going on?' she asked a harassed looking woman at the front of the queue.
'We've run out of food love, every Saturday we have a free supper here for anyone who wants to come. But it's got so popular we can't cater for everyone, and look! This week there's more than ever. I don't know what we're going to do.'
The woman began to smile.
'I know where there's a free party,' she said. 'Lots of great food, lots of good things to do. And no one to enjoy them.'
She stepped into the road and turned towards the growing queue of people.
'Come on you lot,' she said, 'Follow me.'

The Bit Where Dave Explains How to Turn Up at a Party...

People throw parties for all kinds of reasons, birthdays, anniversaries, because they feel cheerful, because they desperately need to feel cheerful, or because their parents have gone away and no one can stop them. Christian parties can be quite different to other parties. Christian parties often include quiet conversations and slim slices of quiche. Teenage parties tend to include loud music and loud vomiting. The music is useful because it covers up the noise in the bathroom. Or in the wardrobe. Or in the rose bushes, or wherever.

The man from Nazareth loved parties. And there may well have been more vomiting than quiche at the ones he attended. The kind of people he befriended were the ones his mother warned him about. 'You don't want to hang around with that Matthew,' she often used to say. So what did he do? Hung around with that Matthew. And went to his parties. You know what teenagers and Messiah's are like, always doing the opposite of what their mum's tell them.
'That Simon Peter's a bit rocky,' his mum probably said. 'Keep well away.'
So, what did the man from Nazareth do? Only went and told him. 'You're rocky,' he said and he didn't keep anything like well away. 'Now that Judas,' his mum would have said one day after school over a huge tea of 5000 fish and bagels, 'now he's a nice boy, his mum told me so. He always dresses well and he's got aspirations. You should spend more time with him. He works hard and he hopes to be famous one day.'
Hmm.

They always say you shouldn't arrive too early to a party. Etiquette dictates that you don't want to appear too keen, or get there in enough time to finish the sausages on sticks before everyone else gets there. You're also supposed to bring a bottle. Usually one that's full. Empty ones don't go down so well, and going home with one that is more full than when you arrived is definitely out of order.

The man from Nazareth pitched up at one particular party having neglected to bring a bottle at all so he made use of a few nearby jars and some bathwater. No one is really sure whether this was good etiquette or not because it had never been done before and isn't in the Good Party Etiquette guide. All we know is that not many woke up in time for church next morning.

At other parties he proved to be downright embarrassing. Like the time he turned up at a wake and promptly ran off with the body. Strictly speaking they both ran off, him and the body, to get extra supplies for the impromptu *Welcome Back to Life* do that subsequently broke out.

Some people are wallflowers at parties, hanging around on the edges. Some people eat wallflowers at parties, usually if there are illegal substances involved. The man from Nazareth went to some quite dodgy parties and got in trouble for it. He didn't get arrested, that would come later, but he was criticised for being too much of a party animal.

There are all kinds of party animals of course, slugs who leave strange trails and don't look much like they're at a party at all, hyenas who insist on singing along with everything, bears who come along with sore heads from the previous party the night before, and the apes, who never come alone. They always bring along their extremely bad habits.

When asked to describe his world, the man from Nazareth said, 'Think of a party so big that it doesn't matter how many people you pull off the streets, there's still enough food and drink for everybody.' And it never ends, which is fortunate. Think of the clearing up afterwards.

Proverbs 9 vv 1-6 & Luke 14 vv 16-20

1 Wisdom has built her house; she has carved its seven columns.

2 She has prepared a great banquet, mixed the wines, and set the table.

3 She has sent her servants to invite everyone to come. She calls out from the heights overlooking the city. 4 "Come in with me," she urges the simple.

To those who lack good judgment, she says,

5 "Come, eat my food, and drink the wine I have mixed.

6 Leave your simple ways behind, and begin to live; learn to use good judgment."

> ¹⁶ Jesus told this story: "A man prepared a great feast and sent out many invitations. ¹⁷ When the banquet was ready, he sent his servant to tell the guests, 'Come, the banquet is ready.' ¹⁸ But they all began making excuses. One said, 'I have just bought a field and must inspect it. Please excuse me.' ¹⁹ Another said, 'I have just bought five pairs of oxen, and I want to try them out. Please excuse me.' ²⁰ Another said, 'I now have a wife, so I can't come.'

The Serious Bit

Jesus loves the idea that God's kingdom is a party, or a feast, or a banquet. He turns funerals into parties, he brings extra wine to a wedding, his followers throw parties, and when asked to describe the kingdom the first word that comes to his mind is 'party'. He doesn't say a temple gathering or a church service or a worship event. He says the P word.

I have had different experiences of parties over the years. Obviously as a child we had jelly, ice cream and pin the tail on anything that got in the way. When I hit my teens we put the lights down, turned the music up and hung onto girls in the dark. Adulthood brought a shock. Parties were now places where you turned the lights up, the music down and hung onto paper plates rather than the other sex. Many of these were Christian parties too, so there was less wine and more lemonade.

I think I preferred the teenage phase. Making out in the dark was so much easier than making conversation in the light. I'm no good at small talk, so it doesn't feel much like a party really. I don't quite know what a party thrown by Jesus looks like, but I don't think it will be a 'Praise Party'. I've been to a few of those too. There's a lot of song-singing and hand-clapping. Ouch. The wise woman in the book of Proverbs gets loads of wine and food ready and my guess is there is plenty of music and dancing in the dark too. Maybe even a live band. One thing's for sure, people will want to come.

The shocking end to Jesus's parable has a second darker sting to it when you couple it with the story people already knew - the one about the wise woman. She threw her party and invited people to come and learn and grow and enjoy the experience. In Jesus's story those people invited – *had not turned up.* The people of God had stayed away. So Jesus had come along to invite lots of other people to this party.

Cheers!

?   ?   ?   ?

The Royal Wedding Scandal
(The Wedding Feast)

Dave's Version

It was uplifting news when Prince William and Kate Middleton decided enough was enough - it was time to get hitched. It was time to get very publicly married. They set the date, mid-spring, when hopefully the weather would be good. They told the press, and put out countless interviews and photos. The country was going through a bad time so, all being well, this would lift everyone's spirits. The crowds would line the streets, the world would turn out, and billions would watch at home on their TV sets. This was going to be big.

Westminster Abbey was booked, invitations were sent out, the dressmakers got busy and all holiday was cancelled for the bodyguards. The day drew nearer and the forecast was... okay. But nothing could stop it now, the wheels were turning and soon the scene would be set for the wedding of the future king.

The day dawned. The soldiers had polished and pressed their uniforms, the caterers had been busy since before dawn, the horses were groomed to perfection. Kate's dress was a work of art and Will's uniform was... okay. Time for the kick off.

But as William and his brother Harry set out for the Abbey the streets were strangely deserted. Tumbleweed drifted past the car. There was no one camping out. No visitors from far flung countries. The people hadn't yet turned out. In the Abbey there were spare seats, only half the choir turned up and they were clearly out of tune. The Archbishop was there and the Queen managed to roll up, but other important dignitaries were missing. Kate appeared and floated down the aisle in her perfect dress and William turned to her.
'You look beautiful,' he said, and she gave him a warm, confident smile. The marriage went ahead and they made their vows.

After the service they climbed aboard the royal carriage. And no one cheered. Because no one had come. No one cared.

As they rode back along the streets William and Kate caught sight of the families and individuals huddled around their televisions, watching Soap Operas and Reality TV, programmes like Cookery on Ice and Strictly Paint Drying.

One or two children ran out of front doors to watch the spectacle and William and Kate did their best to wave, but it was all so bewildering and confusing. Where was everyone? Why had they not come to the best event of the year? Didn't they want to see Kate's dress, didn't they want to witness a double kiss on the balcony? Apparently not.

Will leant over to Kate and whispered to her. No one heard, only Kate. But as soon as they arrived back at the palace a huge number of aids were sent out to invite those who slept on the streets all the time. Those who had not had the chance before to come to a royal wedding. The invitations went out and Kate and Will waited to see who would come.

The Bit Where Dave Explains How to Do the Unexpected...

A good wedding needs three things. A couple of people who'll say 'yes' to the right questions and the right person with a couple of questions. The rest are optional extras. The cake, the crying, the terrible dancing, the excessive handshaking, the long speeches. It's all extra. That said Royal weddings are rarely small occasions. You won't find the Duke and Duchess of Whatever tying the knot in a back street registry office so they don't have to invite mum and dad. You won't get The Prince of Plymouth and the Baroness of Bognor hiking off to Vegas to get hitched at midnight dressed as a couple of cowboys in the chapel of love. Doesn't happen. The words 'quiet' and 'do' don't feature in the Right Royal Family's thesaurus.

Weddings were big in the Bible too. They went on for days, including the slap and tickle bit which well and truly sealed the marriage. Whether you had to slap and tickle louder than usual to impress the crowds listening in on the other side of the curtain is not clear, but the whole village was certainly invited along. Usually the biggest heartache about a big day is whether or not to invite Auntie Ethel and her inappropriate habit. Not so in ye olde Biblical times. Everyone pitched up and the feasting went on for a week. So plenty of snacks were available whilst listening in to the slap and tickle. Just don't crunch those crisps too loudly, you'll put the groom off his stride.

Nowadays one must always send out embossed, decorative invitations in plenty of time. This is so that when people turn down the offer

53

you have just enough time to invite all the second-raters along. Second-raters aren't usually sleeping rough and eating out of a dustbin, but you never know. When the man from Nazareth told his party tale all those first invited turned it down. That meant there was plenty of room for the second-raters, and third-raters, and fourth-raters, and then even Auntie Ethel and her inappropriate habit.

Some wedding receptions have buffets and some have nourishing food. Either way you usually discover you are on the last table to be called or served, even though you are the table nearest the front and you were dead sure when you sat down that you wouldn't have to wait an hour and a half. There's nothing worse than having to watch Auntie Ethel go by with her paper plate piled high with Chinese ribs, French bread, German sausages and English mustard. And then having to watch her inappropriate habit go past after her with his plate piled even higher.

One day, I am assured, there will be a big wedding feast in heaven. And I bet there will be no waiting around. There will be plenty of inappropriate guests though. Which is why I have hope. It means I get invited along.

Matthew 22 vv 1-10

Jesus said, ² 'The Kingdom of Heaven can be illustrated by the story of a king who prepared a great wedding feast for his son. ³ When the banquet was ready, he sent his servants to notify those who were invited. But they all refused to come!

⁴ "So he sent other servants to tell them, 'The feast has been prepared. The bulls and fattened cattle have been killed, and everything is ready. Come to the banquet!' ⁵ But the guests he had invited ignored them and went their own way, one to his farm, another to his business. ⁶ Others seized his messengers and insulted them and killed them.

⁷ "The king was furious, and he sent out his army to destroy the murderers and burn their town.

> [8] And he said to his servants, 'The wedding feast is ready, and the guests I invited aren't worthy of the honour. [9] Now go out to the street corners and invite everyone you see.' [10] So the servants brought in everyone they could find, good and bad alike, and the banquet hall was filled with guests.

The Serious Bit

I have one favourite image from the day of Kate and Will's Royal Wedding. It's not the dress or the cake or even the double kiss (sounds like a game of snooker).

It's the shot of thousands of people making their way through the streets of London to celebrate with the happy couple. When I saw that I saw again why Jesus likened his role to that of being a bridegroom. He's the Biblical Will, come to invite people to this kind of celebration. Crowds of happy people in the streets, moving in one direction to celebrate something good.

And meanwhile, up and down the rest of the country, street parties going on with live music and games and food and drink... the kind of parties where everyone is invited along.

We had no idea then that in a few short months we would see other groups out in the street. Looters and mobsters running amok, destroying lives and homes and businesses. The complete opposite of the crowds on Will and Kate's day. A little like the difference between the huge crowds that pitched out on Palm Sunday and the carefully chosen malicious crowd that lurked in the darkness on Good Friday.

Will and Kate's party crowd came out in the day. The rampaging looters came out at night.
But even in the despair of those few days in August the bridegroom's crowd could still be seen, turning out in the daylight with brushes and bags and the intention to make things better. The intention to bring hope to places broken in the darkness.

Just like Jesus.

? ? ? ?

The Britain's Got Talent Finals
(The Sheep and the Goats)

Dave's Version

A hundred hopefuls lined up yesterday at London's O2 Arena for the start of this year's *Britain's Got Talent* finals. The hundred aspiring contenders waited for hours to audition for this year's big prize. Looking at the line of wannabe stars it was difficult to tell the winners from the losers. They all look so much alike. Outside in broad daylight you just can't tell. Practising set speeches and routines, they were all equally eager, chatty, nervous and impatient, no matter what talent lurked inside their bones. In the short time I was there I met a dozen jugglers, at least twenty singers, a handful of magicians and several troupes of dancers. There was a man with a dog on his head, a boy who could burp all the songs from The Sound of Music, a girl with an ambition to be the first female pope and a whole family of impressionists who could mimic the Waltons, the Simpsons, the Osmonds and the Osbournes.

Come 2.00pm and the curtain goes up – the moment of truth for everyone. One by one they are called and they each step out onto the stage and into the spotlight, hopeful yet terrified. The judges are merciless and scribble their notes as they sort the talent from the dross. The acts perform this, that and the other, and the celebrity panel watch, often aghast, sometimes in wonder, and occasionally with sheer terror. Then hours later, and after a hefty supply of coffee and green room refreshments, the judges return from their deliberations and the hundred reappear on the stage. The crowd must be split now, not all will go through. One by one they are singled out, some go to the left, some to the right. But by the end no one remains in the middle. There is no fence to sit on here. There are some surprises, some broken hearts, and a few angry recriminations. The winners all look relieved and many express their delight and relief. They leave chatting and laughing noisily, a few sparing a last moment to glance apologetically towards the other group. The losers are a quieter bunch. Subdued, some smouldering angrily, they slip off quietly through another door, a different way.

And afterwards there are plenty of reporters to go around, interviewing the winners and losers. Searching for the personalities and the stories behind the acts. The judges stop to chat briefly but don't hang around for long.

Once again I find myself outside staring at the hundred as they make their way home. Once again they look so similar in the daylight, though they have now been divided. Half will be back, half will not.

The Bit Where Dave Explains How to Get Chosen...

The thought of being divided up is never that appealing. Especially if you're a bacon and egg quiche, then the thought of it is just downright carnage. When you're at a school you often find yourself in a line of people who are there just so they can get split up. It's called football practice and what happens is the sports teacher waits until it is raining heavily then invites everyone to stand along a muddy white line while the two best players the school has ever seen walk around dividing the class up. Half will be picked for their ability to kick a ball without falling over. The other half will be picked because the teacher tells you that someone has to have them. The first to be picked then run around madly scoring goals. The last to be picked hang around glumly near the goals, talking about chemistry or a sonnet by Shakespeare. The feeling of not being picked passes though, and soon the boot will be on the other foot, or in fact not on anyone's feet, when it's time for Latin. And booting a ball into the back of a net will in no way help the best players the school has ever seen to conjugate a verb.

Unless they're absolute geniuses as well. Then you're stuffed and that sort of thing really shouldn't be allowed. But let's face it, genius happens.

Twelve men got picked by the man from Nazareth. This wasn't for playing football without falling over, this was so they could lay down everything they had. They weren't so much winners as losers. Two fishermen, James and John made the team which was at first great for them, not so great for their dad who was then two sons short of a fishing team. He had to then pull out his wallet, release a few moths and pay for a couple of new fishermen, preferably a couple who would have made rubbish disciples and would not then be head-hunted by another rabbi.

Simon Peter was the biggest loser in that particular team, attempting to score lots of goals but invariably booting them into the wrong net. He was also skilled at placing both feet in his own mouth. The man from Nazareth picked lots of people to join his team and they were usually the unexpected ones. The ones normally left on the touch line until the bitter end. The man from Nazareth seemed to get confused and often overlooked the best players in the school, instead favouring the timid, the confused, those with sick notes and the ones who yet again had 'left their P.E. kit at home, sir.' No matter. They didn't need their P.E. kit for this team. Just the ability to do things that would turn the world around. Not too demanding then.

To get chosen by the man from Nazareth you didn't have to hang around on a muddy line in the rain. You just climbed a tree or hid in a toll booth or sat by a well in the heat of the day. The kind of things that made you stand apart from the crowd, mainly because the crowd hated you. You didn't have to be smart or witty or rich. But then you didn't have to be dumb, glum or poor either. You just had to be close enough to the man from Nazareth to hear him calling you.

It's worth noting that while a football team is limited to eleven players and a few subs, the Nazareth team has an unlimited number of players and no subs whatsoever.

Matthew 25 vv 31-40

[31] 'But when the Son of Man comes in his glory, and all the angels with him, then he will sit upon his glorious throne. [32] All the nations will be gathered in his presence, and he will separate the people as a shepherd separates the sheep from the goats. [33] He will place the sheep at his right hand and the goats at his left.

[34] 'Then the King will say to those on his right, "Come, you who are blessed by my Father, inherit the Kingdom prepared for you from the creation of the world. [35] For I was hungry, and you fed me. I was thirsty, and you gave me a drink. I was a stranger, and you invited me into your home.

> ^{36} I was naked, and you gave me clothing. I was sick, and you cared for me. I was in prison, and you visited me."
> ^{37} 'Then these righteous ones will reply, "Lord, when did we ever see you hungry and feed you? Or thirsty and give you something to drink? ^{38} Or a stranger and show you hospitality? Or naked and give you clothing? ^{39} When did we ever see you sick or in prison and visit you?"
> ^{40} 'And the King will say, "I tell you the truth, when you did it to one of the least of these my brothers and sisters, you were doing it to me!"'

The Serious Bit

Sheep and goats don't look very alike round here. I live near a valley which is full of them. They don't smell the same either. I'm told that goats urinate on their own beards, so that would make the difference then. However in Jesus's part of the world sheep and goats look remarkably similar, which puts his parable in a new light. The king has to choose between the sheep and the goats, and it's not easy. The differences are small. Sometimes they come down to a cup of coffee, or a short conversation. The sheep are the ones who stopped to care. The goats are the ones who stopped caring. Nowadays I guess the sheep send postcards to those in prison, they support organisations who are working to free slaves and those trapped in trafficking. They buy *The Big Issue*, they send emails to lobby MP's about problems of injustice, they serve in soup kitchens. They help people fill out forms and help them get financial assistance. They encourage others with a smile.

Jesus spent a lot of his time impersonating a sheep. We think of him as a shepherd but he often looked like one of his own followers, caring for the marginalised.

I have just this moment heard that there is such a thing as a geep. Guess what – it's a cross between a goat and a sheep. It's true! I have just googled 'geep' and found Lisa, born in Germany to proud parents – mum the sheep and dad the goat. Apparently goats have a strong sex drive. Strong enough to make them leap fences and take their chances with Lisa's mum. Hmm. I may well be a geep. I certainly have days which are way more goatish than sheepish.

The one thing that the goats and the sheep (or the geeps) can't do is pretend. It's no good them bringing along their Oscars or gold medals or cycling proficiency certificates. The king doesn't need any help, he's astute enough to take one look and spot those who walk the walk, those who talk the talk, and those who limp the limp. I seem to limp more than walk, but I definitely do far more talking than either.

Baaaaa...

?   ?   ?   ?

The Archaeologist and the Thieves
(The Wheat and the Weeds)

Dave's Version

When archaeologist Max Maguire punched a hole the size of his fist through the tiled floor he got the shock of his life. He had found an undiscovered 12th century tomb buried beneath an old Coptic church. Maguire discovered a buried stairwell beneath the Egyptian chapel when he accidentally fell against the font and put his arm through the weakened floor tiles. He watched in amazement as the dust cleared and there before him was the crypt stacked high with piles of undiscovered treasure. Unfortunately others had followed him down there, and the next thing he recalled was the blow on the back of his head. When he awoke two masked figures were sitting in the semi-darkness separating the treasure into two piles.

'Ah, Mr Maguire,' said one, through his mask. 'You'll be pleased to know we won't be taking everything. Some of this is unbelievably beautiful, and some... is dross.'

And as he said this he tossed a tin plate to one side. Max tried to move but he found his arms were tied together behind his back at the elbows and his feet were chained to the ancient stairwell. He could only watch as the two figures separated the treasure.

'Good...bad...good...bad...good ...bad...'

Max thought he detected an Eastern European accent but he couldn't be sure.

'Good...bad...good...bad...good ...bad...'

Two hours later (these men were not rushing their job) they had finished. They bundled the good stuff into a sack and left the other pile at Max's feet.

'Enjoy your share Mr Maguire. You are an archaeologist – everything old is worth something to you – no?'

Then the man stopped, looked in the sack and pulled out a golden chalice. 'I tell you what, we'll not be greedy Mr Maguire. Have one of ours.' And with a laugh he tossed the gold cup onto the pile of cheap tin.

And they went, still laughing and with their boots thumping on the stairs. Max tried to break free to follow them but after hours tied up his body was as stiff as a tree trunk. He was going nowhere in a hurry. He struggled against the ropes but the thieves had done their job well. In his frustration Max kicked against the pile of cheap treasure at his feet. Ironically his foot caught the one piece that was worth something, the chalice. It flew up in the air, bounced off the wall and smacked against Max's forehead. He saw it coming and tried to dodge it but he was too slow. The chalice left its mark.

Dazed, Max slumped back against the wall and glared at the piece of treasure, his head throbbing. He stared at it for a long time, and slowly the truth dawned. Suddenly Max threw back his head and laughed. And it was the laughter that saved him. Somewhere up there, beyond the walls of the church, others were passing and the raucous noise brought them running. Puzzled faces looked down at him through the hole in the floor and before long he was free.

Max rubbed his battered forehead and picked up the golden chalice.
'Look!' he said to the baffled locals, 'look!'
He held out the cup so they could see the mark where it had collided with the wall. The gold had scraped off and underneath the metal was dull and grey. Max hooked up a cheap tin plate and worked on it with his nail. He laughed again.
'See,' he said, though it was clear the locals didn't see. 'They spent all that time separating it out and they took the wrong stuff. Whoever buried this lot down here took the precaution of disguising it. Look, it's not tin, it's gold!' he scraped the metal with his thumb. 'Everything they left behind – it's gold!'
And he threw back his head and laughed again, which was a mistake, because he thumped the back of his head against the crypt wall.
Now that did make the locals laugh.

The Bit Where Dave Explains How to Wait...

It's easy to rush things. You can rush your dinner, or your make-up, or your time on earth. Rushing your dinner will most likely give you indigestion and that bloated feeling you hear so much about in afternoon commercials. Rushing your make-up could cost you a serious proposal of marriage. Or get you one. Rushing your time on earth is a bit like expecting that your life will really start once it's really ended.

Being patient is not easy, especially in the queue at the post office. And sometimes life feels like one long queue at the post office. And there's always someone at the front with thirteen parcels, all different sizes and all going to Outer Mongolia; plus ten pension books and four freezer bags of coppers for changing up.

No one really wants to wait anymore. Fast food outlets have put most of the slow food outlets out of business, pay-as-you-go phones mean that no one wants to pay as you stop anymore and movies on demand have made *movies I never asked for* seem like a joke. Admittedly not a very funny one.

No matter how fast we eat, put on our make-up, run for the bus or choose that wedding outfit, we would all really like things to be better. Most people want their lives to be sorted out, the bad people to be put in a blender or deep fat fryer, and the good people to win the lottery. Every week. Everyone's waiting for that but some of us wait better than others. Some of us don't wait at all and try and sort out life right now, deciding just who the blender-bound bad guys are for themselves e.g. traffic wardens, people who spend all their time in the middle lane of the motorway and Arsenal supporters.

However life is not straightforward, it has bends and u-turns and u-bends and right turns and wrong turns and traffic islands and desert islands and double yellow lines and triple yellow lines and signs that tell us these roadworks will only be going on for another decade. You can't always second guess who is who amongst all this. The good guys could look good but be bad. And the bad guys could smell good and still be bad. The bad guys who are good might actually be bad. So we live in a strange place with all this. I don't mean Milton Keynes, although you may well live there, I mean we live in the now and the not yet and the coming soon and the coming-not-so-soon.

There are days when we might long for the end of all things. Days when we're stuck in that traffic queue/bus queue/post office queue/snooker cue again, or nights when we find ourselves watching Lord of the Rings extended edition. But no matter how quickly we run about with our smart phones and our go-faster stripes on our speedos, the end is the one thing we can't speed up. Oh, and snails of course, pretty difficult to fast track them. So that's two things then, snails and the end. The end - when justice will be done and the things we wish we could rush now, like having to wait at roundabouts and getting rid of bad people, will then and only then be finally sorted out.

Matthew 13 vv 24-30

24 Here is another story Jesus told: 'The Kingdom of Heaven is like a farmer who planted good seed in his field. 25 But that night as the workers slept, his enemy came and planted weeds among the wheat, then slipped away. 26 When the crop began to grow and produce grain, the weeds also grew.

27 'The farmer's workers went to him and said, "Sir, the field where you planted that good seed is full of weeds! Where did they come from?"

28 "'An enemy has done this!" the farmer exclaimed. "Should we pull out the weeds?" they asked.

29 "No," he replied, "you'll uproot the wheat if you do. 30 Let both grow together until the harvest. Then I will tell the harvesters to sort out the weeds, tie them into bundles, and burn them, and to put the wheat in the barn."'

The Serious Bit

Jesus tells a couple of stories about seed growing. In one of them not much happens: the farmer sows some seed, goes to bed and has a good night's sleep. The he gets up, has a wash, cleans his teeth, has breakfast and does a bit more work. Hardly a thriller is it? And yet, Jesus says, something extraordinary is happening while the farmer's ordinary life goes on. The seed is growing, and the farmer has no idea how it's happening. He doesn't need to understand it to make the miracle work. You can find that story in Mark chapter 4 somewhere around verse 26. 'The earth,' says Jesus, 'does its own work,' thank you very much. Once the seed and the soil have shaken hands the rest is up to life itself.

Cut to this parable, the one where the unlucky farmer gets ambushed. Compared to the mundane nature of the other story this looks like a Spielberg movie. Bad guys turn up and invade the field and – shock horror! – plant things!!

When Jesus strolled into town at the start of Mark's gospel he invited the people to repent. The Greek word used there - metanoya - doesn't mean fall on your knees, weep and say sorry for your sins. It means 'think again'. It means change your mind. You see, the locals were waiting for the Messiah, and they knew that when the Messiah came the oppressive Romans would be kicked out. Well, here comes Jesus but the Romans are not going to be leaving town. The Messiah has arrived and is bringing with him the seeds of the wheat of God's kingdom, but the Romans, the weeds if you like, they are not going to be pulled up. God's kingdom will grow, in ways we don't understand and can't predict, and it will do so alongside the bad things in life. At times there is conflict and at times the wheat overpowers the weeds, but most of the time you find both in the field.

The worst assumption that we can make is that to be a Christian means all our problems are solved. The wheat and the weeds grow side by side for now. God's kingdom is breaking into your life, and it will bring good things, but the difficult parts of your life will most likely go on. Because that's the way the Messiah has chosen to work for now.

Not easy sometimes.

?   ?   ?   ?

The Not-so Secret Millionaires
(The Talents)

Dave's Version

Alan Sugar launched his new Saturday night game show last night, and he is literally throwing money at people. In The Not-so Secret Millionaire three lucky contestants each get given £5000 to see how they can increase it. In last night's pilot programme, Larry from London, Jill from Plymouth and Dev from Bolton did their level best to barter, gamble and sweat their way to a fortune.

Larry rented a market stall and set up in business selling a strange mixture of watches, underwear and DVD's. His suppliers wished to remain anonymous but he did a roaring trade and was pretty soon looking like one happy salesman.

Jill went into business with her close friend Shirley, setting up their own kebab takeaway in the centre of the city, just down the road from the local nightclubs and cinemas.

Dev took the biggest gamble of all, investing in some fire sticks, carving knives and a decent guitar he booked himself a square in Covent Garden and set out to fulfil his lifelong ambition of becoming a successful street entertainer.

Three weeks later and the three hopefuls limped back into the TV studios, all dragging huge bags of cash. Larry was all grins and no underwear. He'd sold the lot, along with all his watches and DVD's. He was a very rich man indeed, and Lord Sugar said so. Good Larry was going to get his own permanent stall and make a mint.

As was Jill. She had done all right too. The late night fast food trade had been a roaring one. A mountain of meat had been transformed into a cascade of cash.

Dev was lugging the biggest sack of all. He tipped out the contents and there was an audible gasp in the studio. A huge pile of damp, muddy fire sticks, knives and musical instruments sat there dripping rainwater and slug-slime. He'd started well, got a bit of a crowd on the first day, but didn't make much money. This was going to be a slow process and by day three he'd lost heart. The public had not been generous and as he watched Larry and Jill's businesses take off he knew he'd made a mistake. He couldn't make it work. So he took his stuff, shoved it in a big hole and hid it for a while. Hoping it might all go away. Then he went home and crawled into bed, wishing he had thought of underwear and kebab selling. 'At least,' he said, 'I've brought it all back. I haven't lost any money, there's still £5,000 worth of kit here. You can trade it in.'

Lord Sugar was not happy. Not happy at all. And he said so. Dev had wasted his money and his time.
'You could have at least banked the cash, even with the today's rates I'd get a little something extra back. Dev,' he said, 'you're fired.'

The Bit Where Dave Explains How to Take a Gamble...

There are many kinds of gambling. Businessmen do it on the stock exchange. School kids do it behind the bike sheds. Sheep do it - usually behind the dipping sheds. Lambs are particularly avid gamblers, but then that's no surprise, gambling can often turn into a teenage problem.

Certain kinds of gambling are frowned upon, using other people's money to place a bet for example, or betting your grandmother on the Grand National, that kind of thing. Other things are frowned upon too, like picking your nose in public and eating the result. In some cultures fingers are preferred to handkerchiefs but no one really wants to share a finger buffet in those particular places.

Some say that you can't get anywhere in life without taking a gamble. Certainly this is true of getting on the underground in London. Who knows where you'll end up with closures on the Bakerloo line and replacement buses on the Circle. Risky experimentation affects other things too, our diet for example. Every time you open a Kinder Egg there's a surprise in store. And there's no telling what you might find when you bite into a fast food burger. We've asked, but there's no telling so we just assume it's edible, we know it's not healthy but we trust it's edible.

Down the ages food has been a source of severe gambling. Before poker or Russian roulette were invented people used diet as a way of taking dangerous but thrilling risks. We would still be eating raw grass and tree bark had the early cave people not experimented with sautéed potatoes, sole meunière and chicken tikka masala. Indeed many cave dwellers died in the course of developing the recipes for

the first cook book, The Semi-Naked Chef. We owe it to them that
Sweet 'n' Sour Arsenic and Pork Tartar in a White Spirit Sauce were
dropped from chapter three.

'Businesses grow in an atmosphere of risk and gambling.' So said the
Earl of Earl's Court, now bankrupt. But it is easier to play it safe, to
bury what you have in the garden and go off and watch daytime
adverts for Claims Direct. No one really wants that, unless you're
Alan Titchmarsh in which case whatever you bury is likely to come
up smelling of roses. And looking like them too. But burying your
talents is rarely a good idea. Even in a hermetically-sealed
Tupperware box your money is not going to grow and your talents are
just going to sit there in a plastic cash bag.

Better to take a risk and make a few mistakes and learn as you go.
Most brain surgeons did it this way, and even if they did end up
burying a few things as a result, they became proper doctors in the
end!

Matthew 25: 14-30

[14] 'Again, the Kingdom of Heaven can be illustrated by the
story of a man going on a trip. He called together his servants
and gave them money to invest for him while he was gone.
[15] He gave five bags of gold to one, two bags of gold to
another, and one bag of gold to the last—dividing it in
proportion to their abilities—and then left on his trip. [16] The
servant who received the five bags of gold began immediately
to invest the money and soon doubled it. [17] The servant with
two bags of gold also went right to work and doubled the
money. [18] But the servant who received the one bag of gold
dug a hole in the ground and hid the master's money for
safekeeping.

> ¹⁹ 'After a long time their master returned from his trip and called them to give an account of how they had used his money. ²⁰ The servant to whom he had entrusted the five bags of gold said, "sir, you gave me five bags of gold to invest, and I have doubled the amount." ²¹ The master was full of praise. "Well done, my good and faithful servant. You have been faithful in handling this small amount, so now I will give you many more responsibilities. Let's celebrate together!"
> ²² 'Next came the servant who had received the two bags of gold, with the report, "sir, you gave me two bags of gold to invest, and I have doubled the amount." ²³ The master said, "Well done, my good and faithful servant. You have been faithful in handling this small amount, so now I will give you many more responsibilities. Let's celebrate together!"
> ²⁴ 'Then the servant with the one bag of gold came and said, "sir, I know you are a hard man, harvesting crops you didn't plant and gathering crops you didn't cultivate. ²⁵ I was afraid I would lose your money, so I hid it in the earth and here it is."'

The Serious Bit

This is a great parable if you're competitive. Jesus here is encouraging a 'Dragon's Den' approach to using your skills and gifts. Who can do well? Who can make the best of what they have? I spend a lot of my time looking over my shoulder at what others have and can do and I end up feeling insecure and impotent. I have lived in various communities in the last 25 years and I found this to be a tough challenge. I became acutely aware of the many talents I don't possess, to the detriment of appreciating the talents I do have.

Everyone can do things, everyone is unique, it's just – to coin a cliché – some people seem more unique than others. For example I have never really been into sport. I'm a fair-weather armchair supporter – if Team GB or England's ball-kickers, golfers or tiddly-winkers are doing well than I'll get involved. I tried being a dedicated Leeds United supporter as a boy but it didn't last. (Some may well blame my choice of Leeds as evidence of my sporting inability.) I tried but I just couldn't get into it and I was hopeless at propelling a ball around. As a bloke that can be soul-destroying and intimidating. I recently started kicking a ball around with my 9 year-old-daughter and her friend. I actually enjoyed it and managed to not look like Mr Bean. At 48 I have finally found my footballing level.

It's dead easy to look at others, take a jaundiced view of your own talents and bury the whole lot for a long time. One of the most difficult things is to be yourself, to be happy with what you have, and to make good use of it. I was chatting last night with a friend who told me that one understanding of Paul's quote that we are not fighting against flesh and blood but against authorities and powers – is that we fight against the systems of the world. Systems that can be selfish and destructive. Jesus is asking us to see ourselves and the world differently. To respect ourselves and others, and to use our gifts to bring life and hope the best way we can, not aping what others can do.

No weakest link here.

?   ?   ?   ?

Local Hero
(The Good Samaritan)

Dave's Version

Last night a man was recovering in hospital after being set upon by a gang of malicious thugs. Police are looking for the gang and also the mysterious woman who delivered the man to the hospital.

The man, named only as Joe, nearly died when he was mugged late on Tuesday evening, on his way back from a night-club in the centre of town. He was walking back along a quiet country lane when he was attacked by a gang armed with knives and bottles. This is the third incident of this kind in the last two weeks. The young man was left beaten and bloody and lying in the middle of the road.

A truck driver, two bikers and at least four cars all went past before the young woman stopped her four by four and climbed out to help the man. She used a first aid kit from the car to patch him up as best as possible before hauling him to the car and laying him across the back seat.

She then climbed in to drive him to a hospital and found that the engine would not start. After several attempts she gave up and climbed out. She then called for an ambulance and waited, but none came. The young man then described how she stood in the middle of the road attempting to flag down passing vehicles. Eventually a man on a Harley Davidson pulled up. She flicked open the bonnet of her car and persuaded the stranger to have a look at the engine for her. The man appeared reluctant but he eventually took a look.

After several attempts to fix things the car would still not start and the stranger was in the process of getting back on his Harley when the woman pulled him back. She pressed him to take the man on the back of his bike to the local hospital. When he refused she produced her wallet and handed over an unknown sum of money. The stranger nodded and hauled the man onto the Harley. The girl took a photo of him and the bike with her phone to ensure he kept his word and then she proceeded to call the hospital with the news that they were on their way.

The biker delivered the man to the hospital and left immediately without a word. The beaten man caught his first close look at the biker's face as he hauled him into the hospital reception. He was too dazed to say anything to the man.

Police are keen to track down the girl, not only so the mugged man can thank her, but also because she has a photo of one of the gang. It turns out that the Harley owner was one of the thugs who had originally mugged the man.

The Bit Where Dave Explains How to Be a Hero...

Helping people is no bad thing. Helping them cross the road, helping them carry their shopping, helping them cut the grass. However, it's worth checking beforehand that they actually wish to cross the road, that it's their own shopping they're running home with and that the grass in their garden is completely legal.

Even small acts of kindness can make you a hero. However acts of random kindness can not. This is mainly because such acts don't exist and annoy the pants off the grammatically correct pedantics of this world. I know this because I am one and let me assure you that no matter how kind you have just randomly been to that three-legged dog with the stammering woof, it's not the kindness which is random - it's the act. I think we've got that straight then.

Being a hero is never easy. And sometimes the most un-heroic people can turn out to be heroes and the heroic-looking ones don't. Heroes are often selfless. When the chips are down it's the heroes that pick them up, dust them off, add vinegar and share them round. The un-heroes just send out for more fish. The man from Nazareth was a hero but not in the normal sense. Unlike Superman he did not wear his pants over his tights. In fact he did not wear tights at all. He didn't have a batmobile, a cape, a whip or the ability to spin spider-webs from his wrist. Any hero having all these qualities would certainly be worth inviting round for a sherry.

The man from Nazareth certainly covered the saving the world bit, but not by fighting The Green Goblin, The Joker, Magneto, Lex Luther, Sinestro, Dastardly and Mutley or Toilet Duck. Instead he battled those dark villains of night known as The Pharisees and The Sadducees. Marvel Comics have yet to produce their First Century Temple Scoundrels edition, but one day they will and all will be revealed.

72

He also battled other enemies, the likes of loneliness, pride, selfishness, greed, arrogance and rejection. Not easy to fight because they all have cloaks of invisibility. So they move around silently, taking their victims right in front of our noses. The man from Nazareth unmasked these reprobates with his compassion and cunning, with his wit and strange stories. Like the one about the mugged traveller. Being a mugger should never be confused with being a mug, which is an entirely different thing altogether. However, those dastardly Sadducees and Pharisees managed both. They mugged the poor with their extortionate temple tax and then got exposed as mugs by the man from Nazareth who frequently stopped by the roadside to help the poor muggees.

Samaritans in general were never heroes. They were smelly people from a nasty place who everyone could happily dislike without any fear of political incorrectness whatsoever. A bit like politicians and bankers today. Only the man from Nazareth held them up as being better than Batman, Spiderman and Superman put together.

Matthew 10 vv 30-37

[30] Jesus told them an illustration: 'A Jewish man was travelling on a trip from Jerusalem to Jericho, and he was attacked by bandits. They stripped him of his clothes and money, beat him up, and left him half dead beside the road. [31]"By chance a Jewish priest came along; but when he saw the man lying there, he crossed to the other side of the road and passed him by. [32] A Temple assistant walked over and looked at him lying there, but he also passed by on the other side. [33] "Then a despised Samaritan came along, and when he saw the man, he felt deep pity. [34] Kneeling beside him, the Samaritan soothed his wounds with medicine and bandaged them. Then he put the man on his own donkey and took him to an inn, where he took care of him.

> ^{35} The next day he handed the innkeeper two pieces of silver and told him to take care of the man. "If his bill runs higher than that," he said, "I'll pay the difference the next time I am here."
>
> ^{36} 'Now which of these three would you say was a neighbour to the man who was attacked by bandits?' Jesus asked.
>
> ^{37} The man replied, 'The one who showed him mercy.'
>
> Then Jesus said, 'Yes, now go and do the same.'

The Serious Bit

Some parables are easy to talk about. This has to be in the top 3 most discussed, along with the prodigal son and the two builders. Easy to discuss – but actually doing it? Now that's another story. I recall hearing the actor Tom Conti being interviewed on the radio. During the show someone called in to say that Tom had recently helped their mum carry a huge pile of shopping out of the supermarket. Tom may well have been embarrassed but I was impressed. Actions matter, don't they? Words can be relatively cheap really. Politicians and religious leaders have said much over the years. Twitter, Facebook and YouTube are stuffed full of people like me making easy comments. A lot of talk.

Kindness is not cool but it is courageous. And sometimes it's naïve. Jesus's story has a certain naivety to it. Samaritans were not only hated people, they were enemies. And this was bandit country. In a drama workshop once I asked the folks taking part to create new versions of chosen parables. One group chose the Good Samaritan. When the Samaritan stopped to help the injured Jew the man on the ground suddenly leapt up and beat the living daylights out of the Good Samaritan. Deeply shocking - and it happens.

But of course being a Good Samaritan is not only for these extreme occurrences. You have probably already re-enacted this parable once or twice today. There is any number of possibilities in any given day. I have quoted this before, but I never tire of passing it on. Shane Claiborne once said, 'Get ready, because God is preparing you for something very very...

small.

Because it's small things that change the world.'

Go for it.

?   ?   ?   ?

Marty Hicks and the DJ
(The Persistent Widow)

Dave's Version

After years of trying Mrs Susan Hicks finally got her request played on national radio.

Mrs Hicks first sent in a request for her son's birthday 43 years ago. When the day came and went without the song being played and her son being mentioned Mrs Hicks was heartbroken. So the next year she tried again. She was still overlooked. So she tried the following year. Still no success, but Mrs Hicks refused to give up. She and her son had a difficult life, her husband having been killed in a mining disaster. They had had to battle the odds and persistence had become Mrs Hicks's middle name. She continued with her efforts, every year sending in bigger, more colourful cards. She sent photos of her son, along with various pairs of his football socks, in various states of cleanliness. She framed and sent a lock of his hair, along with copies of his birth certificate, cycling proficiency award, and the third place certificate he won in the school long jump.

Year on year went by and plenty of other sons got a mention, but not Marty Hicks. Marty left school went to college and then got a job. But his mother refused to give up, if anything her determination grew. She baked cakes and sent them in, she posted sausages on sticks, stew and dumplings in padded envelopes, and apple pies with cash bags full of custard. She sent pictures of his wedding day, along with a slice of cake. Then a video of his daughter's Christening along with more cake. With the dawning of the internet she taught herself how to use email, then Facebook , then Twitter, solely so she could keep sending in her requests. Every year she listened in, and every year there was no request played. The DJ's career rose and fell over the years, he went from the breakfast show to the drivetime show to the lunchtime slot, finally ending up on a late night weekend show.

And still it went on - the food and the pictures and the messages kept coming – with no response.

Until yesterday.

Yesterday, nearly half a century after she began, the DJ, Adrian Puffin, finally picked out her request.

'I had no choice,' he said, in an interview afterwards, 'there were no other sons left to play songs for. It was nothing personal,' he said, 'but we can't play everyone. At first she just got overlooked, then she became something of a nuisance, then a bit of a joke. But in the end Mrs Hicks's persistence become downright irritating, I was starting to hallucinate about seeing more and more pictures of her son and I was having very bad dreams about her. I'd wake up screaming in the night. Though, I have to say, through it all - she was a great cook. Nobody bakes apple pie like her.'

Let's hope the 53-year-old Tim Hicks enjoyed her song choice - *On the Good Ship Lollipop* by Shirley Temple – it was the original song she has been requesting every year ever since she began.

The Bit Where Dave Explains How to Not Give Up Easily...

It used to be said, 'If at first you don't succeed then try again.' Thankfully Guy Fawkes had never come across this one. Robert the Bruce once sat in a cave and watched a spider spin a web repeatedly and got all inspired. Most people sit in their houses watching spiders spin webs repeatedly and get all depressed. Cobwebs may be the product of perseverance but reaching up into dark corners with a duster has caused many a slipped disc and split underpants.

Abraham Lincoln may not have done much dusting but he didn't give up either, in spite of a hard life and many disappointments. He started his working life acquiring a shop on credit, he ended it running the country as the 16th president of the USA. That's perseverance. Nowadays or course, you can get a whole country on credit. But that's another story. Many people have to battle the odds to win through. Butterflies have to fight their way out of a cocoon just to get a life. Rather like the way the rest of us have to fight their way out of a Tesco's car park just to get a life.

The president of Remington shavers was so taken with his personal fuzz buster that he went down in history with this particular outburst: 'When my wife bought me a Remington shaver,' he said, 'I was so impressed I bought the company.' That's not so much perseverance as bragging. There are thousands of stories of people who have battled the odds and not given up. But you won't find them in OK magazine. Glossy photos and nice white teeth are more appealing to those of us who have to battle hard every day just to switch off the alarm clock.

Praying is one of those things which require perseverance, in fact it could be said that there's not a lot of point starting to pray unless you're in it for the distance. Praying is a long haul flight, not a two-minute trip on the tube. Although it can feel as uncomfortable as both. Praying is a marathon - it's not a 100 metre sprint. And it's not either of them when it comes to gold medals. You don't get awards or medallions for keeping up knocking on heaven's door year after year. You can get sore knees though.

Praying doesn't really fit the quick fix culture. There is no microwave equivalent of praying. No spiritual concord available. These days of course there's no physical concord either. Praying may break the sound barrier though. Many have beaten on the floor and torn their clothes and screamed at the sky for assistance... as they sit impatiently in overcrowded airports. Others have learnt the technique whilst sitting impatiently in undercrowded churches. Praying is free. You can pray anywhere in any language for any length of time. Apart from some Cathedrals where you have to freely donate the required charge to get inside.

But you don't need to be in a cathedral to pray, you can do it anywhere. And you don't need to get sore knees or a floor to beat upon or some clothes to tear. The man from Nazareth prayed outside, inside, upside and downside. His prayers were all over the place. My prayers are all over the place too, but in a slightly different way. The good news is that you don't have to be good at praying. And you don't have to be the president, a spider or a marathon runner. You just have to keep having a go.

Luke 18 vv 1-8

1 One day Jesus told his disciples a story to illustrate their need for constant prayer and to show them that they must never give up. 2 'There was a judge in a certain city,' he said, 'who was a godless man with great contempt for everyone. 3 A widow of that city came to him repeatedly, appealing for justice against someone who had harmed her.

> [4] The judge ignored her for a while, but eventually she wore
> him out. "I fear neither God nor man," he said to himself,
> [5] "but this woman is driving me crazy. I'm going to see that
> she gets justice, because she is wearing me out with her
> constant requests!'"

The Serious Bit

I pray a lot of prayers and then forget. I forget I have prayed them and I forget to keep on praying. I know I forget because occasionally other people remind me or I write them down in a little notebook and then I rediscover them at unexpected moments. I guess this is a little different if you are praying for something vital and significant - like freedom from a dictator. You may well pray for that every day. Or if someone you love is sick. You can't help but pray for these things as often as you can.

There is another story about Jesus that is almost the opposite of this. A man comes to ask for his son to be cured. He prays a desperate prayer to Jesus, he says, 'Please do something if you can.'
Jesus encourages the man to have faith and the man replies, 'I do have faith, but I also have doubts, please help me.'

On other occasions Jesus is frustrated by peoples' unbelief, but not here. Here he understands and honours the man's honesty. I like this prayer: 'Please do something if you can'. Let's be honest with Jesus. We are not always like the persistent widow. We are not always full of faith and able to keep on knocking, asking and searching. Sometimes we can only pray our small, hopeful prayers. And Jesus understands.

He himself prayed several prayers that have not been answered in two thousand years.
'Father,' he prayed one day, 'please may my followers be united.'
Ah. Bit of a snag there. He'll have been thinking about the church when he prayed that. The church that invented the rack and the thumbscrew so we could torture one another over theological disagreements.

I think he understands that prayer is not easy.

?   ?   ?   ?

Three Thieves - One Burglary
(The Thief in the Night)

Dave's Version

Once there were three people living in three houses in a rich part of town. And there were three thieves who were planning to break into these three houses and steal everything. The first thief waited until eight o'clock, pulled a balaclava over his head and tiptoed down the garden path of house number one. He found an open window and slipped inside. Then he crept into the lounge and got a shock, because the owner, a sweet old lady called Mrs Alice Lert, was sitting inside with a shotgun, two rottweillers, a mobile phone and a stick of dynamite. The moment he broke in she called the police, held him at gun point, put the dynamite down the back of his trousers and got the rottweillers to sit on his feet until the cops arrived.

Fortunately she didn't injure him in any way otherwise she'd have gone to prison for twenty years.

The second thief waited until nine o'clock, then he pulled a gorilla mask on his head, and tiptoed up the garden path to house number two. He slipped open the kitchen window,

climbed inside and also got a shock. The owner, a gentle ex-nun called Miss Viper Sharp, had been taking karate lessons and as soon as the thief landed in her kitchen sink, she put him in an arm lock, flung him over her shoulder, swung him round by the neck, tied his feet around his elbows and knocked him out with a karate chop. When he woke up he was in a police cell with back ache, head ache, leg ache and bottom ache.

She was in the cell next to him hoping he wouldn't press charges.

The third thief put a David Cameron face mask on his head, tiptoed up the garden path, then tripped up on his way as he couldn't see a thing. He tried to prize open a window but broke his crowbar as he was doing it. So he smashed a very big and loud hole in the front door and walked in through it. Inside he helped himself to the TV, the DVD, the Wii, the Wi-Fi, the hi fi, the X box, the beatbox, the iPad, the iPod, the CD collection, the complete works of Shakespeare and the fridge. He carried them all outside in one big pile and put his back out on the way. Then he loaded up his van, and drove off, accidentally knocking the greenhouse down as he drove through it.

But in spite of all his bungling, the third thief got away with a fortune, because the owner of the house was Mr Bean, and he had sent his guard dog to the vet, his shotgun to the menders, his telephone to the cleaners and he'd taken up origami instead of karate lessons.

And when the thief came Mr Bean was out somewhere, making the Eiffel tower out of two paper napkins and a Neighbourhood Watch flyer.

The Bit Where Dave Explains How to Be Ready...

Getting ready for something is often more important than the thing itself. A social do can last for a couple of hours but the planning can last a couple of days. No one wants to turn up at a fancy dress do dressed for the opera, and no one wants to go to a vicars and tarts party dressed for church. Unless you're a vicar, then I guess you're okay.

You can't always be ready for an unexpected guest, you don't normally have that down in your diary. And thieves are even worse. No one has that in the diary - except the thief of course. He or she has an organiser full of dates when they'll be turning up at your house. They just haven't let you know yet. They will let you know... you'll get the news about an hour after they've been.

Maybe if they had a website called *Thieves Are Us* they could post their busy schedules up there and you and I could sit at home with a few beers, some Doritos and a copy of Home Alone in the DVD player ready to entertain them as they help themselves to the silver and the rest of the DVD collection. It would make life easier for the police too. They could compare diaries and cross-reference them with the bad guys.

'Tuesday? Mmm...we already got two break-ins that night. How does Wednesday look? Thursday? Yep. That works for us. Love to, we'll be there. See you then. Oh, do you prefer handcuffs or plastic ties? And uniformed or plain clothes arresting officers? Okay, Got that. Great.'

No thief in the universe is going to turn up if they know the cops are waiting in the wings. Unless there's forty of them and they're appearing with Ali Baba in panto in Woking. Likewise no homeowner goes out, knowing that there's a bunch of local crooks working in the area. Except when they're a bunch of cowboy painters and decorators doing up the house next door. Any self-respecting homeowner makes sure their house is secure and protected with a canine in every kennel and a camera in every corner.

Any fun-loving criminal is going to then be photographed from every angle and bitten in every bottom. They won't be rushing back in a hurry. Or even limping back at a gentle stroll.

The man from Nazareth is no thief, or a cop. But he does come unexpectedly and the date's not always in the diary or posted up there on *Messiahs Are Us*. Or rather *Messiah Is Me*. So best just to keep the old eyes peeled and the ears pinned back and the other three senses tuned too. Then when he rolls up like that thief in the night you'll be ready with the Doritos and the cheery welcome.

Luke 12 vv 42-48

39 'Know this: A homeowner who knew exactly when a burglar was coming would not permit the house to be broken into.

40 You must be ready all the time, for the Son of Man will come when least expected.'

The Serious Bit

The thought of always being ready for Jesus can make me feel scared and tired. This idea that we must always be on alert is not unlike guard duty in the trenches in the First World War. If you were caught napping, dozing off to sleep, you could be court-martialled there and then. And if found guilty you could be shot the next morning. Serious stuff.

I'm not very good at staying awake, yet this story can make Jesus sound like a tyrannical sergeant major, waiting to pounce on us weary soldiers if we should lean on our rifles and start to drop off. Must stay awake, must keep watch, must stay awake, must keeeeeee...zzzzzzzzzzzzzzzzzzzzz.
Too late.

This isn't the only parable Jesus tells about watching out. There's the one about the bridesmaids - the ten girls who run out of oil.

They are waiting for the groom and only five of them are ready with their lamps when he comes. The others have to run and get a refill and when they get back the groom says, 'Sorry... don't know you.'

Er. Rrrright. Makes a lot of sense doesn't it... doesn't it? I thought bridesmaids were supposed to wear a lot of make-up, get their hair done, carry bits of the bride's dress and fight to catch the bouquet when she throws it away. Haven't ever seen them running about chasing oil. Even though there is a shortage these days.

A few years ago we went to a friend's wedding in France. She and her husband had the legal proceedings done at an office, whilst we went to the church to be ready for their arrival for the service. I have never waited so long for a bride (and groom) to arrive. Obviously French weddings are more relaxed than English. They took forever! I think I'd brought a book with me (I often take a book to church) so I had something to read, but it was such a long wait. Apparently, in some cultures, not only does the groom stop off on the way to the wedding, but they have the ceremony at night – which is why bridesmaids need lamps and oil.
So, the bridesmaids wait, they doze off, and only some of them have planned for the long, hard wait and still have oil to light the streets for the groom when he comes.

There are wise and foolish women in the book of proverbs, and they both advertise their lifestyles, trying to persuade others to join them. Jesus's story about these wise and foolish women may not be so much about staying awake to watch for the return of Jesus. After all, all of the girls doze off to sleep. Instead this is a story about lifestyle, living as people who are on the king's side. Ready and waiting for him by following his lifestyle. Some of the girls in this parable have not kept their focus, the others have, following Jesus for the long haul, through the good times and bad, through success and failure, through faith and doubt.

?   ?   ?   ?

The Mochachino of Hope
(The Unproductive Fig Tree)

Dave's Version

A failing restaurant got a helping hand last night when, on the brink of closure, an anonymous businessman offered to bail it out. A spokesperson for the generous benefactor said this: 'My boss has always loved this restaurant, though it has been going downhill lately. He grew up in this neighbourhood and has happy memories of coming here for meals with his family. When he heard it was on the verge of closing he felt he needed to give it one more chance. Hence the generous financial arrangement.'

Rumours abound about who the benefactor is, some say it's the local judge, others that it's a movie star, others that the owner has somehow persuaded the bank to help out. Still others claim there is no benefactor it's just a scheme to get publicity and curry extra business.

A press release promises that the restaurant will get a face lift, a revamped menu, and some extra staff to help lift it out of the doldrums. Live entertainment and the wall space for local artists to display their work is also promised as part of the new lively look.
'My boss has done this before,' said the spokesperson, 'he enjoys reviving failing businesses and turning them around. He relishes the challenge.'
And if this venture fails?
'Well, he can't prop it up forever. He says he'll give it a year and see what happens. If it hasn't turned around by then he'll have to pull the plug. He'll be very sad to do that, because as I said, he loves this place, but he's a realist. He knows that it's a risk but he's willing to try and give the place a chance. So we wait and see.'

The Bit Where Dave Explains How to Get Second Chances...

Some things never offer a second bite of the cherry. Cherries for example - most are just too small to offer themselves for a bite a second time, all you can do is shove the whole lot in and watch out for the stone. Key birthdays also, like eighteen and twenty one, if you miss those they don't come round again a few years later. And

England winning the football world cup. That only comes around in 1966. After that? Nope, may as well take up water-polo or competitive sneezing.

However lots of other things do offer second chances. Like education; if you mess around and waste the first eighteen years of your life, don't worry, you can always do an Open University Degree in Aztec Child Sacrifice or Incan Vandalism. All is not lost. Or dying your hair - if you're not happy with your natural red then blonde is only a bottle away. Jeans can be returned to the store and cars can be traded in. Children too can be exchanged... oh no, not children. Sorry, got carried away there.

Driving tests offer multiple chances. A woman in Slough has taken hers 132 times. The series of tests have become more like a regular date for her, she fears her life may actually fall apart if ever she were to pass and go out alone without L plates or a driving examiner. Her local test centre would be in danger of going out of business too.

We all need second chances. If you couldn't have another crack at trying Guinness, coffee, black pudding or watching an Agatha Christie these things would no longer be with us. Agatha Christies often require multiple chances. It may always be the butler, but why? And which one is the butler? And what exactly did he do anyway?

The man from Nazareth was big on second chances. His own nation had not exactly come top of the medals table in the 'performing well as a benign and stranger-friendly bunch' competition, but he had high hopes. One day they might turn into Colonel Sanders, it was just a matter of time. How much time was the problem. Right now they resembled Basil Fawlty and it was all taking a little bit longer than expected to get them back on track.

It was once said that the main thing is to keep the main thing the main thing. The man who said it is now recovering in a psychiatric ward, but he had a point, albeit a convoluted one. Many of us begin with the main thing and then find lots of lesser things, tiny things, minuscule things, to worry about. The main thing about second chances is that most of us get them and therefore most of us can pass them on. You can't wrap one up and put it in a shoebox with the labels removed and a ribbon added, though that would be useful. And if someone ever gets a website up and running offering this, I'll have a dozen please. At the moment all we can manage is to have a supply ready when we and anyone nearby needs to pick themselves up, dust themselves down and try again.

> ## Luke 13: 6-9
>
> [6] 'A man planted a fig tree in his garden and came again and again to see if there was any fruit on it, but he was always disappointed. [7] Finally, he said to his gardener, 'I've waited three years, and there hasn't been a single fig! Cut it down. It's taking up space we can use for something else.'
> [8] The gardener answered, 'Give it one more chance. Leave it another year, and I'll give it special attention and plenty of fertilizer. [9] If we get figs next year, fine. If not, you can cut it down.'

The Serious Bit

This must be close to the top of the obscure parables chart. Certainly, given a choice between preaching on the prodigal son or this one I know which way most preachers will go. But it is more encouraging than it might first appear. It has to be understood in the light of older parables, and for that just flip back to Ezekiel the prophet who loved stories about vines. The main thing about the vine is that it's kind of Israel's nickname. So in chapter 15 Ezekiel says, 'This vine? It's rubbish. Not even useful for making a good fire.' In chapter 17 the vine goes looking for water and sustenance in the wrong places and as a result, there's no mercy for it. It's destined to be pulled up so it can wither and die. Things are not looking good for Israel, this is hardly the kind of thing you want to read in your horoscope in *Hello Magazine*. Two chapters later the vine story has been turned into a funeral song. Oh dear.

But here comes Jesus – he knows Ezekiel's stories but he's brought a new one, one that doesn't necessarily end in destruction and disaster. There is hope here. The man wants to pull up the vine, or the fig tree, but the gardener won't let him. 'Give it another chance,' he says, 'there's still time for it to grow and flourish.' And this is the same gardener who says, 'Get connected to me and you will bear fruit. Without me you can't do anything. But with me all things are possible.'

'Let's see.'

? ? ? ?

The Impossible Dream
(The Servant and the Master)

Dave's Version

One night a man had a dream that he came home from work to find the Prime Minister on his doorstep. He let the minister in and the politician made him a cup of tea and switched on the Xbox for him. The Chancellor of the Exchequer then appeared and gave him a handful of free money, and the housing minster arrived and announced that he'd brought him a brand new home on the expensive side of town.

Jamie Oliver then rolled up to cook him his favourite meal, Jeremy Clarkson arrived in a Lamborghini and handed him the keys, Guy Ritchie called and offered him half a million to star in his latest movie and Johnny Depp skyped to see if he wanted to go down the pub.

The pub landlord had just poured him the perfect pint when somebody rang a huge bell in his ear. It was 6 a.m. time to switch off the alarm, get up, get showered and dressed, assemble the kids' packed lunches, make his wife a cup of tea, walk the dog, unblock the downstairs toilet, then jump on the train and head for work. Just another day in paradise...

The Bit Where Dave Explains How to Be Realistic...

We all have dreams. Some of them are repeatable and we'd love to have them every night. Some are unrepeatable and we can't possibly tell anyone about them. Some of them feature people we like, some of them feature people we'd like to be, and some of them featured people we'd like to be barbecuing. Whether or not it's summer. One thing's for sure, we can't control our dreams any more than we can stop laughing in a library when something is unintentionally funny.

Dreams can be frustrating. For example we may get rich and be popular in our dreams, we may be the perfect husband, wife, father, footballer or safecracker. But in reality we all wake up in the same mess every morning, with the pillow wrapped round our head and the duvet missing presumed stolen by the wife/

husband/dog again. We all of us muddle through life getting a lot of things wrong most days, apart from the safecrackers. They can only get it wrong once, after that they're eating prison food for a while dreaming of nothing but freedom.

If you or I were to come home and find everyone waiting on us hand and foot we would probably jump to the obvious conclusion, that we have finally been rumbled, someone found out that we have no chance of ever paying off the mortgage and so someone else richer and with better prospects has bought our house whilst we've been out at work. We do work hard but don't expect to get rewarded at home by our wives, kids, servants, slaves, concubines or dogs. We do what we do because it's good and right. And we're saving for that speedboat.

The man from Nazareth knew that we understand how life works. 'Don't get your hopes up,' he might say, 'Johnny Depp is not going to buy you dinner. He might come up with his own line of Hollywood pies and try and sell you one - a kind of movie tart - but he's not going to buy one for you.'
It's no use doing a hard day's work in the hope that the great and the good will be waiting to give you a Bafta and a round of applause when you get home. Likewise, don't bother doing stuff for the Creator so that you get a big reward. Much better to do it out of gratitude. A humble heart is better than a proud foot. Or liver. Or left earlobe.

There will not be a bunch of Celestial Charlie's Angels sitting on your garden fence swinging their legs and singing *I Will Always Love You* when you crawl home tonight smelling of blood, sweat, tears and the tube.

Doing good things for God is not unlike doing good things for your guinea pig. He'll be grateful and really pleased and eat up all that cucumber - but he won't necessarily give you a hug or buy you a new DVD. Apparently other people are his weapon of choice for urging you on. So you need that wife/husband/er... dog(?) who stole the duvet in the wee small hours to do that for you. Or a friend who didn't.

The Serious Bit

This parable seems hard. Why can't I come in and put my feet up and be waited on. Life is difficult. Being a Christian is demanding. I deserve a little 'me time'.

Israel made a big mistake in Old Testament times. It got confused about the meaning of the word *chosen*. It thought that this meant they deserved special treatment, that they were better than everyone else. They had it right and everyone else was wrong and deserved punishment. In reality they had been chosen all right – chosen to serve the world. Chosen to demonstrate the life and compassion of God, chosen to live differently so that others would be drawn to the light of God. They were chosen, for example, to not have a king. But they looked at other nations and decided they wanted a king. So they stopped being different.

The danger for us in the church, in the body of Jesus present now in the world, is that we make the same mistake. We can think we have been chosen because we are *better*, we are special, we are right and everyone else is wrong.

Jesus invites his disciples to follow him. To follow a rabbi means spending time with him so that you become like him. And this rabbi is different. He doesn't just teach with his stories, he teaches with his lifestyle. He cares for people, he is humble, he is hopeful and witty. He enjoys and celebrates life, and he refuses to assert his authority by putting others down. And then he says to us, 'Follow me, learn from me and have a go yourself.'

Does going to church on Sunday sometimes feel like the servant coming in, putting his feet up and expecting the Master to wait on him? I'm not sure, perhaps it does. Perhaps we think it should do. Serving the world can be exhausting. What best helps and inspires and equips us to keep following Jesus?

Only you can answer that.

?   ?   ?   ?

Another Runaway Boy
(The Prodigal Son)

Dave's Version

The search continues for the missing schoolboy Tom Blue. Sixteen-year-old Tom left home on 14th February and has not been seen since. Describing him as difficult at home and arrogant at school, neighbours say this is not the first time Tom has run away, but he has always returned within a day or two. The boy has now been gone three and a half weeks. Fearing the worst, his parents have appeared on television giving their heartfelt plea for his return, or for any news of his whereabouts. There has been no demand for a ransom of any kind or any other information submitted regarding the boy, but the police say they cannot rule out abduction or foul play.

A boy matching his description was seen boarding a train for London three weeks ago and a bag of discarded clothes similar to those worn by Tom Blue was uncovered in a ditch yesterday morning, but the police have no further information on this. Posters have been placed all over the city and friends and relatives have begun a Facebook campaign in an attempt to track him down.

Tom's brother Paul appeared sullen and angry when interviewed last night. 'He's just seeking attention,' he snarled at the press, 'he's always doing this. He doesn't care about anybody else, he ran off 'cause he wanted his own way. And now look, he's got everyone falling over themselves to bring him back. He'll be living it up somewhere with some tarts and a few gangsters, having a right laugh. Trust me, the idiot'll come limping back when he's ready, you wait and see. When he's broke and nobody cares anymore, then he'll switch on the charm and come back with a little set speech about how he's terribly sorry and please can we all forgive him and let him come home and start again. Jerk.'

The Bit Where Dave Explains How to Run Away...

I only recall running away from home twice. Once when I was about 12, the other when I was 27. If you're serious about leaving it's best to pack a suitcase, preferably one with wheels, a lunch box with your favourite sandwiches, a giant pack of Doritos, your iPod, your laptop and your kindle... then wrap them all up in a blue and white spotted handkerchief and tie it onto a knobbly stick which you're sure to find by the back door.

I didn't do any of that. I stormed out in a strop, with no careful planning whatsoever. So I was carrying nothing useful when I stomped out of the house and up the road and pretty soon I couldn't think of anything else to do. So I ran out of steam, sat down on a low wall by the road and stewed in my own juices for a while. Probably apple or pineapple juice, they were always my favourite. Not orange or grapefruit, best to only have those if you have a cold and need the vitamin C. Funnily enough the running away experience was pretty much the same whether I was 12 or 27. I left when I was 12 because I was frustrated and didn't want to eat my peas. I left when I was 27 because I was frustrated and didn't like the people I was living with. Peas you can reheat or throw away. You can't do either with other people. Well you can, but a prison sentence usually follows.

Yourself and other people just don't mix. John Paul Sartre once said, 'Hell is other people'. Probably not the best guy to get trapped in a lift with for 48 hours. You can't control other people, they don't come with a little remote and a spare set of batteries. So sooner or later they do something downright unreasonable, like closing the door at the wrong volume, and you have to blow up at them and wish them the worst future-life anyone could ever possibly have. Not long after that you might decide to leave.

The best piece of preparation to do if you're going to run away is your returning home speech. You can plan that weeks in advance with no cost to your credit card or even using up valuable time. You can plan it whilst watching TV or eating a nutritious meal like sugar and crisp sandwiches. Make it as contrite as possible because not many people are likely to take you back in if you walk through the door with a list of demands as long as the Magna Carta.

Motives on returning are usually mixed. You may well feel deeply sorry about abandoning everyone else and making them worry for 5 hours, and because you left with the DVD remote in your back pocket.

But you're also likely to be hoping that they'll enjoy your set speech, give you a hug and a hot meal and perhaps even nominate you for an Oscar. The boy in the man from Nazareth's story returned stinking to high heaven. You don't really need to go that far, depends how bad you've been. This boy had been a little on the reckless side. Stealing his inheritance money amounted to wishing his old man was dead so he promptly slipped off the top spot of his family's most popular son list. Indeed his older brother was leaning heavily towards wishing his younger sibling dead and was seriously considering making his wish come true.

But at the end of the day - love conquers everything. Or in this case, the smell, the pig dung down the trousers and the complete lack of Lynx under the armpits. The old man made everybody cringe by throwing himself at his son, knocking him backwards and sending the two of them rolling down the street together. It may have taken a little while for the runaway boy to realise he was being welcomed and not throttled, but either way his set speech was wasted, he never got more than a few sentences out.

He did get a big party though, and huge wodge of forgiveness, even though his brother was still highly miffed, and last seen packing a big blue and white spotted handkerchief with his iPod, his laptop and his kindle.

Luke 15 vv 11–18

11 To illustrate the point further, Jesus told them this story: 'A man had two sons. 12 The younger son told his father, "I want my share of your estate now before you die." So his father agreed to divide his wealth between his sons.

13 'A few days later this younger son packed all his belongings and moved to a distant land, and there he wasted all his money in wild living. 14 About the time his money ran out, a great famine swept over the land, and he began to starve. 15 He persuaded a local farmer to hire him, and the man sent him into his fields to feed the pigs.

> ¹⁶ The young man became so hungry that even the pods he was feeding the pigs looked good to him. But no one gave him anything.
>
> ¹⁷ 'When he finally came to his senses, he said to himself, "At home even the hired servants have food enough to spare, and here I am dying of hunger! ¹⁸ I will go home to my father and say, 'Father, I have sinned against both heaven and you, ¹⁹ and I am no longer worthy of being called your son. Please take me on as a hired servant.'"

The Serious Bit

If I had a pound for every time I've heard this parable I'd have £143-72. It goes around and comes around like an episode of *Dad's Army*. It's familiar and cosy and comforting.

It wasn't like that when Jesus told it. It was offensive and shocking and loaded with barbed humour. Any story that began with the line 'There was a man with two sons...' immediately reminded the public of their own story. They were descended from a man with two sons. His name was Isaac, and his son Jacob is their distant relative. When the story goes on to describe the younger son leaving home then they are convinced. This *is* their story. Jacob left home, went to his uncle Laban's, got married, became rich, had a big family, came home and was reconciled to his brother.

Jesus knows this. He knows their expectations, that's why he's telling this story. He wants to mess with their minds. He wants to show them that Jacob has not turned out the way he should have done. So Jesus's story takes some unexpected twists and turns. The prodigal doesn't get married, he sleeps with prostitutes. He doesn't make his home with his uncle, he feeds with the pigs. He doesn't come back surrounded by his own children, he limps up the road alone. He doesn't return filthy rich, he just comes back filthy. And there's no tearful reconciliation with his brother – just an ambiguous sibling outburst that hangs in the air like a bad smell. There is some good news though, another strange difference. Isaac is not mentioned much in the original story of reconciliation. But the father in Jesus's story is a key player. He runs like an idiot, like no Israelite father would run. He can't wait to see his son again and is not much interested in any plea bargaining or promises of better behaviour. He just wants to welcome the boy home and bring him back to life again.

However, there were so many shocks on the way many people may not have been able to absorb this unusual picture of a father who is counter-cultural. They may have still been reeling or laughing or scratching their heads at the rest of Jesus's story. They may have needed to hear this story several times for the penny to start dropping. Sometimes it has a long way to fall.

So much has been said about this parable I will just leave you with a thought from Henri Nouwen from his book *The Return of the Prodigal Son*. The father does not want either son to remain the same. He wants them both to do some growing up. Ultimately the invitation is to become like the father, forgiving, compassionate, generous and welcoming. Not easy for either brother, the hedonistic young one, or the legalistic older one.

Where are you on that one?

? ? ? ?

England Ex-Specs
(The Speck and the Log)

Dave's Version

Clem England caused a world of trouble yesterday when he tried to retrieve a lost contact lens. The lens belonged to his lifelong friend Mike Johnson and Clem was concerned to rescue it for him so that he could read the menu in a local restaurant. However, there were a couple of problems. The first problem was that the lens was in his friend's eye. It had been displaced and the lens had moved around and was lodged securely under his eyelid. Mike could not dislodge it himself so Clem got involved. Clem took his rather large finger and did his best to dig around and pull out the flimsy lens. And this brings us to the second problem. Clem is himself long-sighted and couldn't see much of what he was doing.

As a result he poked his friend so hard in the eye that Mike fell backwards off his seat, arms flailing so wildly that he knocked a tray full of glasses from a passing waiter. The contents smashed all over a family celebrating thirty years of marriage, covering them in a mixture of Guinness, sweet sherry, blackberry juice and red wine. The husband of the family leapt out of his seat so quickly that his chair flew backwards into a pregnant women who promptly went into labour. The baby was born amidst the stream of soft and hard drinks, delivered, incredibly by the partially-sighted Mike Johnson, who it turned out, is a local GP in the next village. He delivered the eight-pound boy with one eye closed which only proved what local residents had always claimed - that Mike was such a good doctor he could do the job with his eyes shut.

When asked afterwards why he didn't have glasses to improve his vision, Clem England said that he did, but he didn't think he needed them really. Mike, on the other hand, he said, was very much in need of optical assistance.

The Bit Where Dave Explains How to Judge Other People...

It's probably best to sort out other people. I mean it's more manageable. No point aiming at a target you can't hit. It's easier to put a band aid on your brother's paper cut, than to bandage the gaping, festering wound in your own leg. It's easier to apply a cold compress to his twisted ankle, than it is to reset your own dislocated shoulder. It's more straightforward to pass him a tube of antiseptic cream for his scrape than to amputate the gangrenous bit of you that smells the place out.

And anyway, amputation is painful and noisy and requires some sort of bin for disposing of the clinical waste afterwards. Whereas - if you're brother, or sister has a more manageable problem, (and let's face it, they probably both need sorting out), then solve that for them. Tell them how wrong they are and what they need to do about it, and if they can't fix it today then just keep on until three weeks on Tuesday when they finally sort themselves out. Either by fixing their minor problem or punching you between the eyes. Either way you'll probably not mention the issue to them again.

It's also much less painful and more satisfying to have a go at them for that annoying habit, than it is for you to correct the truckload-load of dysfunctional behaviour in your own repertoire. It's a much better idea to point out their faults and have a go at their failings than to take a long hard look at yourself in the mirror and acknowledge what you see.

If we're honest it may be time we all did a little slowing down when it comes to the fast lane of criticism, to wake up and move out of self-denial. When it came to the talent queue for mistake-making and clanger-dropping there was no queue, it was more like a Beatles concert with everyone jammed at the front. We were all first in line, no one got served last.

Sometimes we avoid mirrors because of that shaving cut, or that spot on the nose, or the blonde hair colour that turned green in the swimming pool last week. Whichever, it may be time to grin and bear it, take a good long look at ourselves and tell ourselves we are not the person to play judge and jury for our next-door-neighbours. We did that when we were ten, and look how badly that turned out. Tears, tantrums and grounded for a week. No one needs that kind of fuss when they're old enough to cut themselves shaving or dye their hair greeny-blonde.

Somehow we all end up with the gene, the 'why-can't-you-just-sort-yourself-out-a-bit' gene. Not to be confused with the man in baggy trousers who comes out of the bottle when you rub against it too hard. That's a jolly green <u>genie</u> and he gives you three wishes. The other kind is a judging gene and that's what comes out when you rub up against a human being too hard. And then you get three insults. Shame we can't just put that gene in a bottle and jam the cork in really hard.

Matthew 7 vv 1–5

¹ 'Stop judging others, and you will not be judged. ² For others will treat you as you treat them. ²Whatever measure you use in judging others, it will be used to measure how you are judged. ³ And why worry about a speck in your friend's eye when you have a log in your own? ⁴ How can you think of saying, "Let me help you get rid of that speck in your eye," when you can't see past the log in your own eye? ⁵ Hypocrite! First get rid of the log from your own eye; then perhaps you will see well enough to deal with the speck in your friend's eye.'

The Serious Bit

I never cease to be amazed at my ability to judge others whilst overlooking my own faults. It's really quite remarkable, I'm very good at it. I'm not sure if I have a special gift for it. Fortunately I also have this little voice that occasionally points out my arrogance and stupidity to me. Hopefully no one else can hear it otherwise I'm in big trouble.

This is a rare kind of parable for Jesus – he's actually drawing on his own experience rather than the experience of his listeners. He rarely tells carpentry parables, usually they are about fishing or farming or widows or shepherds. Jesus is very concerned that people tune into his stories, so he has clearly spent time watching and listening and gathering information about their lives. It would be easy at times to think Jesus was a fisherman or a shepherd because he uses these analogies so much. But he wasn't - he was a builder. We call him a carpenter but I'm told that the lack of wood around those parts indicates that he would have been involved with construction work in general. The nearby city of Sepphoris was enjoying a boom time and being rebuilt so he may well have worked there with his dad. Never heard of Sepphoris? For the record, bibleplaces.com claims that it was also known as Autocratoris, Diocaesarea, Eirenopolis Neronias, Le Sephorie, Saffouriya, Safuriyah, Safuriyye, Seffarieh, Sephoris, Sippori, and Zippori. For all these names Sepphoris is never named in the Bible. Jesus didn't go there once he began his work as a rabbi; he went to the ghettos instead.

This parable is a cartoon in many ways. You can imagine a sketch of this guy wandering around oblivious to the huge plank jutting out of his eye. The Monty Python guys would have had a ball with this. Many of the parables work like that, Jesus stretches a point so that it is funny and unforgettable.

Get the point?

?   ?   ?   ?

Like Father Unlike Son
(The Two Sons)

Dave's Version

On my recent travels I heard a story about a man who had two sons. The younger son came to his father one day and said, 'I want my share of our inheritance now, instead of waiting until you die.' So his father agreed to divide his wealth between his sons. A few days later this younger son packed all his belongings and took a flight to a distant land, and there he wasted all his money on wild living. When he got back he was broke, embarrassed and filthy. His father called the two boys into his study, the older one would not stand near his brother, partly because of the smell, but mostly because of his anger with the way his brother had acted.

'I have a request,' said the father.
'So do I. Can you tell him to have a bath?' said the older son.
'Yea, please can I have a bath dad?' the younger one said. Their father smiled.
'Soon,' he said. 'Now...'
'But dad he stinks!' said the older brother.
'Soon,' said the father.
'No. He stinks now!'
'I do dad.'

The father stood up and walked quietly around the desk. The smell was very bad, a mixture of stale cigarettes, alcohol, urine and vomit. The father came close to his son and did not blink.
'First,' he said, 'I want you to go out into the far field, there's a cow sinking in the swamp there. She will die if you don't go and rescue her soon.'
'Oh not that swamp!' said the older brother. 'It's disgusting. It's like a cesspit.'
'Exactly,' said the father,' now do you see why it's better to do the job before taking a shower?'
The younger son nodded quietly and slipped out of the door. The older son didn't move.
'I'm not going,' he said, 'let him do it. He's already covered in excrement and it'll be a good price to pay for what he did with your money.'
Then the older boy stormed out, slamming the door as he went.

Two hours later the two boys returned. The younger had washed and shaved and cleaned up. The older boy was still covered in cow dung.

'Now who smells bad?' said the younger boy.
'You do,' said his father. 'you stink. I asked you to rescue the cow and you went and washed instead. The animal would have died if your brother hadn't changed his mind.'
The younger boy protested.
'But he said...'
'It doesn't matter what he said, it's what he did that counts.'

The Bit Where Dave Explains How to Do the Right Thing...

King Chulalongkorn of Siam had 33 sons. That's one for every day of the month, if you can't count too well. At one point 11 of them were all at Eton. I wonder if any of them were rebels? There's an old saying that actions speak louder than words. I know what it means but words can get pretty loud sometimes, especially if you use a loudhailer. And some actions make very little noise at all. Opening a door for a stranger won't break the sound barrier, even if it hasn't been oiled lately, and smiling at an enemy will be downright silent unless they punch you on the nose as they pass by.

It's easy to promise to do things and then not follow through. Every time we hand over a fiver we promise to pay the bearer on demand the sum of five pounds, even though most of us don't carry five pounds of gold about our person when we're out for a swim. Most people would be a huge disappointment to the leisure centre receptionist if she started demanding we make good on our promises.

If our actions really could speak they may give us away sometimes. Imagine the response for example, if whenever we nipped off to the loo, our body started a running commentary. 'Dave is now hurrying to the bathroom, Dave is now unzipping...' I think you get the picture. Likewise our secret eating habits would be shouted from the rooftops. Literally. 'DAVE'S EATING THREE BARS OF DAIRY MILK AGAIN. ALL ON HIS OWN - KING SIZE.' And goodness knows how people would react if they knew I regularly watched... well... you know... 'DAVE'S WATCHING LOOSE WOMEN. AGAIN.'
Reading that back I realise that, taken in the wrong way, this actually looks a lot more dodgy than it really is. Although most people admit that daytime TV is the opium of the masses these days.

It would of course be of little use if our words were quieter than our actions. We'd be communicating as if we were in a library all the time, or wandering around the Tate Gallery, or trying not to wake Grandma from her much-needed, before-lunch snooze while listening to a dull sermon.

Many of us are 'Yes people'. Which is not so much to say that we love 70's prog rock, but that we find it hard to say no. This makes it difficult to follow through on all the things we say 'yes' to - cleaning the car, making the world a better place, voting for the Green Party; those kind of things. And before you know it we have a list of things we've promised which, when unravelled, would go round the circumference of the earth three times. Better in the end to say 'no' to most things and then surprise people by actually doing something. Like getting out of bed for example. Or becoming Archbishop.

Matthew 21 vv 28-31

28 'But what do you think about this? A man with two sons told the older boy, "son, go out and work in the vineyard today." 29 The son answered, "No, I won't go," but later he changed his mind and went anyway. 30 Then the father told the other son, "You go," and he said, "Yes, sir, I will." But he didn't go. 31 Which of the two was obeying his father?'

The Serious Bit

This is the parable which strikes at my heart. This is the one that exposes my hypocrisy. I have to hold my hands up and say I'm nicked. It isn't what you say, it's what you do that counts. The older boy says all the wrong things but then relents and does something. The other boy says all the right things and does nothing.

This is also my frustration with Sunday church. It's a place full of the right words, in songs and prayers and sermons. I'm not saying that those who sing and speak and pray are not then following through and living it all out, it's just that I can't. I can't make those grand claims and agree with some of those idealistic lyrics when I know that I am a pale imitation of a good Christian. Most of the time I am that younger boy. I promise to do what Jesus asks, and then I don't do it.

There are other times when I refuse to do the good thing and then find myself relenting and actually doing something worthwhile, but these are not frequent enough I fear.

The thing I do love about this parable is this. There are many people who cannot, for various reasons, say the right words. Life has knocked them about, people have hurt them, they have been disappointed. So they find it difficult to say the things that we expect committed Christians to say. Yet when you look at their lives it's a different story. They are like the older brother, and their actions speak louder than their words.

Sometimes I wonder whether we put too much emphasis on saying the right things as Christians.

Talking, not walking.

? ? ? ?

A Portal to Another World
(The Ladder)

Dave's Version

Scientists are on the verge of a major breakthrough. A possibility so astounding, so shocking that it is sure to provoke worldwide interest and outrage in equal measure. Using a principle nicknamed cross-reality-travel they have pioneered a technique for moving from one realm of life to another. Already speculation and suggestions abound about the possibility of travelling from this world to the spirit world. Scientists are adamant though that the portal they have created is not so much about transporting people from one reality to another but rather a link which will draw two worlds together. Not so much an escape exit, as many would like, but a rope bridge that links the two.

'A rope bridge is a good analogy,' says Deacon Whitecoat, the chief scientist working on the project,

'because this will be a flimsy experiment for a while. The first people to try it, the guinea pigs if you like, will need courage and an adventurous spirit. We are sure that there is another world, or another half of this world waiting to be discovered, a shadow of this reality. But the journey there may be precarious for a while. What we are trying to do is to bring these two worlds together.'

Some religious groups are already accusing Dr Whitecoat of playing God, but he assures them he is himself just being a vehicle, creating a tool which can benefit everyone. 'And like any tool,' he says, 'it could be used for good or ill.'

Those keen to book a ticket for the ride needn't rush. Dr Deacon predicts this door will not be open fully for a while. 'Patience is of the essence,' he says.

The Bit Where Dave Explains How to Break a Code...

Escaping is attractive to most of us. Especially if you live in a castle called Colditz. People are eagerly watching developments re space travel in the hope that we can find another piece of the universe where we can avoid the neighbours, escape the in-laws and dodge the meteorites that are forever passing within a hairsbreadth of this planet. Pie-in-the-sky when we die is one thing, but Pie-in-the-sky while we're still alive would be even better. People used to think the moon was made of cheese but if Mars is a giant pork pie that'll do nicely.

The man from Nazareth often spoke in riddles, by which I don't mean he used to walk around saying, 'Why did the Pharisee cross the road? To avoid the beaten-up man on the other side.' Although he did have a few one-liners like that. But no, he often described himself and the world using ancient mysterious language. Ladders and angels and the son of man are all part of a certain kind of lingo, a coded message, not unlike the ones spies hanging around behind newspapers use, when talking to one another.
'The rain in Spain falls mainly down the drain.'
'Yes, but hamsters wear overcoats when the sun shines out of the back of my head.'
That sort of thing.
Leave you bewildered by any chance?

A runaway called Jacob once had a dream about angels going up and down a ladder into the world of heaven. It told him one thing, he was asleep. But it told him something else too, he was getting a coded message which told him that God was on his case. The Ancient of Days was lurking somewhere nearby and had a healthy interest in him. God hiding in the bushes? Well, it was possible. Later on Moses bumped into the Creator in some desert foliage. Jake had long shuffled off the planet by that time, but from there on any references to ladders and angels were always going to hint at the same thing, God was nearby.

The man from Nazareth used another coded message, the name of the son of man. The son of man was a virtuous man of action and a figure of justice, James Bond, Indiana Jones and Judge John Deed all rolled into one. According to this picture the angels don't need ladders now, they clamber in and out of heaven on the shoulders of this son of man. And if angels are sitting on the shoulders of this particular figure then God is lurking nearby. So, the hunt is on, just who is this mysterious son of man?

Most people think of heaven as paradise in the sky, a sort of Bahamas beyond the ceiling. And we all want to go there. Forget that big pork pie called Mars, let's get away to that heavenly Hawaii. But if the man from Nazareth is to be believed, this other world, this kingdom, this religious reality has come very close indeed, so close that the

son of man is a link, a conveyor belt, a travelator between the two.
Heaven and earth have shaken hands, slapped each other on the back
and given each other a not-so-high five. And the son of man is the
go-between.

Is there pie in that there sky or are their slices of it littered nearby,
in bushes and houses and workplaces and yes - restaurants?
Do we go to heaven or does heaven come to us? Only the mysterious
son of man holds the answer...

John 1 vv 47–51

47 As Philip and Nathanael approached, Jesus said, 'Now here
is a genuine son of Israel - a man of complete integrity.'

48 'How do you know about me?' Nathanael asked.
Jesus replied, 'I could see you under the fig tree before Philip
found you.'

49 Then Nathanael exclaimed, 'Rabbi, you are the Son of God -
the King of Israel!'

50 Jesus asked him, 'Do you believe this just because I told you
I had seen you under the fig tree? You will see greater things
than this.' 51 Then he said, 'I tell you the truth, you will all see
heaven open and the angels of God going up and down on the
Son of Man, the one who is the stairway between heaven and
earth.'

The Serious Bit

Do you ever speed-read bits of the Bible? Skim over them because
you just don't get them? I realise now that I did this for a long time
with this particular weird and wonderful bit about the angels going
up and down on the Son of Man. At mime school (yes, I confess, I
went to mime school) we once did an exercise where one person
stood still while another tried to climb all over them. I have visions
here of winged men in white clambering over a mysterious figure.

Of course this message is a coded one, this is like Jesus sidling up to Nathanael in a car park in Zurich and murmuring, 'The rain in Spain falls mainly down the drain.' And immediately Nathanael perks up and knows he's made that vital contact. The Son of Man is a phrase Jesus has pinched from the book of Daniel. He appears in chapter 7 coming to earth in the clouds and he then becomes king or president over the whole world. Forever. Now what's quite something. Jesus says that Nathanael will see this mysterious figure soon and there will be angels all over him. Angels going up and down on this stairway to heaven. That's reminiscent of Jacob of course, and angels in the Bible signify the presence of God.

So this is shocking stuff. Jesus is hinting that before long Nathanael is going to get a glimpse of the presence of God. Forget Jacob's ladder, there's a new stairway in town, a new link between heaven and earth.

I like this conversation, I like the way Jesus communicates covertly. Jesus is being creative, culturally relevant, covert and cryptic. He leaves a trail of clues for Nathanael to follow, but Nat must work it out for himself. Jesus paints a picture, makes a little YouTube clip, sends a little text message... and the rest is up to Nat, to watch and listen and work it out.

There is a very important reason why Jesus operates covertly of course. The wrong information in the wrong hands will get him killed. So he won't throw his pearls before swine. He will carefully lay his trail of clues and he will pray for us as we find them and work out who he is.

Spotted any lately?

?   ?   ?   ?

To Feast or Not to Feast
(The Bridegroom)

Dave's Version

Dear Sir,

I am writing to complain about the standard of service and catering at my cousin's wedding, held at your hotel last week. The food was cheap, the staff rude, the music cheesy and the wine was like the discarded contents of our tropical fish tank after the cats been at it. When I mentioned this to your manager he laughed it off and promised that things could only get better. I was incensed by the cheap remark, but not at all prepared for what he later dubbed 'Plan B'. No one in their right mind would have done what he then proceeded to do. He waited. I didn't know he was waiting, I thought he was bluffing, but no. Once the party was in full swing, and the guests were completely out of it on the cheap wine and fermented food, dancing like Mr Bean to the Birdy Song, he then summoned a whole new set of staff, who looked, sounded and operated like the A team from Buckingham Palace. A hundred times more professional than the initial rabble. These then proceeded to bring out the kind of banquet that was then wasted on our guests who were themselves so wasted by then they wouldn't have known a chipolata from a Chippendale. The appalling DJ was replaced by the best live band I've ever heard and the party continued for the rest of the night and into the following day.

Is this standard policy for your establishment, because frankly, I'm appalled.

Yours in anger,

Ann Robinson

The Bit Where Dave Explains Fasting and Feasting...

The thing about bridegrooms is that they throw parties. Or they get a wedding planner to do it for them. Either way you get to go to a place where there is food, drink, dancing and good times. And sometimes paper plates. Paper plates can mar the good times of course, try balancing a pint of John Smiths, a handful of bacon and shrimp canapés and a paper plate full of mountainous French bread and

Indian curry and you'll know the meaning of the words culinary nightmare. But flimsy crockery aside, bridegrooms are mostly good to be around. Especially if you're around one that can turn bad times to good, enemies to friends and water to wine.

The man from Nazareth went to at least one wedding, probably dozens of them, as all his village would pitch up at anything that had four legs and a couple of 'I do's'. The one wedding we do know he went to is often mentioned at ecclesiastical ceremonial knot-tyings even to this day, though he wasn't there necessarily to promote marriage so much as generosity and a nice glass of red wine.

One thing you don't do is spend good money on expensive wine for people who are already six glasses short of a trifle. A party well in full swing doesn't require the stuff of legend in a bottle from 1793. Blue Nun will do nicely thanks. Forget the Burgundy brewed by Napoleon, bring out the tripe from Tesco's: that'll do the job. Unless you're making a point about the good life. If you want to demonstrate the generosity of God you won't get far with a stale biscuit and a half a cup of lukewarm coffee. Better to make a splash and lay on the kind of alcoholic river folks will still be talking about 2000 years later.

The opposite of feasting is of course fasting. Mind you if you have appalling manners and eat very quickly you'd just be feasting fast really. Which is not the same thing. Fasting requires restraint and strength of will, and no food. Eating is definitely out. No point going to a wedding where they've laid on extra food and saved the best wine till last if you're trying to cut down a little for a few days.

People fast for all kinds of reasons and it mustn't be confused with dieting. Dieting is where you replace a lot of good tasty food with a lot of bad tasteless food so that you don't want to eat much of it. Usually cabbages are involved. And if that's the case nobody else wants you to eat much of it either. When the man from Nazareth was around the main purpose of fasting was to show that things were not right and you wanted them to be better. Which is why the man from Nazareth didn't fast. He'd come to make it better, to be a bridegroom and wedding caterer for everyone. No point fasting when you're the answer to people's longings. Time to put the 'e' back into fasting and start feasting for a while.

Nowadays we have both in church. Fasting as a prayer and feasting as a celebration. Though often the feasting is just a tiny crumb of bread and a mere sip of wine. Those are the times when we could really do with the bridegroom and miracle wedding caterer showing up.

John 2 vv 1-10

[1] The next day there was a wedding celebration in the village of Cana in Galilee. Jesus's mother was there, [2] and Jesus and his disciples were also invited to the celebration. [3] The wine supply ran out during the festivities, so Jesus's mother told him, 'They have no more wine.'
[4] 'Dear woman, that's not our problem,' Jesus replied. 'My time has not yet come.'
[5] But his mother told the servants, 'Do whatever he tells you.'
[6] Standing nearby were six stone water jars, used for Jewish ceremonial washing. Each could hold twenty to thirty gallons. [7] Jesus told the servants, 'Fill the jars with water.' When the jars had been filled, [8] he said, 'Now dip some out, and take it to the master of ceremonies.' So the servants followed his instructions.
[9] When the master of ceremonies tasted the water that was now wine, not knowing where it had come from (though, of course, the servants knew), he called the bridegroom over. [10] 'A host always serves the best wine first,' he said. 'Then, when everyone has had a lot to drink, he brings out the less expensive wine. But you have kept the best until now!'

Mark 2 vv 18-19

[18] Once when John's disciples and the Pharisees were fasting, some people came to Jesus and asked, 'Why don't your disciples fast like John's disciples and the Pharisees do?'
[19] Jesus replied, 'Do wedding guests fast while celebrating with the groom? Of course not. They can't fast while the groom is with them. [20] But someday the groom will be taken away from them, and then they will fast.'

The Serious Bit

I have never been that grabbed by the image of the church being a bride. I mean, I don't fancy the outfit really. And it seems to me that the purpose of a parable is to draw you closer to the meaning of the story. So the parable of me being a bride, well... hmm. Me and an awful lot of other guys in the church are left wandering in a desert there... However I recently discovered a couple of helpful clues. Firstly – there is actually a reference in the Bible to us being like a groom. Isaiah sends us a quick text about the way that God has dressed us up in decent clothes, a perfect outfit, he says – like a bridegroom decked out in his wedding suit, or a bride in lots of jewels. There you go, that's more like it.

A few verses later (we're talking chapters 61 and 62 here) Isaiah's back on the other image saying that God is well-chuffed with his people, and will celebrate over them like a groom celebrating over his gorgeous bride. This image of God being like a bridegroom is all over the Good Book. It just won't go away. Why? Well, bridegrooms offer so many great things. They invite us to an event which is full of good stuff, food, drink, partying, celebration, relationship, hope for the future and promises made to one another. This is the point of the parable. God invites us to all of this.

He doesn't want us to see him as a powerful dictator, or a cruel father, or a manipulative leader. He wants us to see him as the man about to start a whole new life. A man on the verge of so many good things. He offers us the invitation to join him, with the hope that we'll say those two magic words.

'I do.'

?   ?   ?   ?

Top Yapper Comes Clean
(The Vine)

Dave's Version

We gathered in the pub last night for a rare treat – a local boy made good. All kinds of rumours had been flying around and no one was a hundred per cent sure he would even show up. But come the hour, come the man, and there he was – Jack Chapel - the number one Yapper. I think we all expected a giant of a man but he looked very much the same as he ever did. A little rough if anything, frayed around the edges a bit. He sat on a bar stool at the front with his iPad on his knee and in his quiet, assured voice he gave us some exerts from his recent Yaps. The heavens didn't open and there were no thunderbolts, just that steady, confident delivery. Then, just when we thought it was over, he dropped the bomb.

'Many of you have been following me on the social network known as Yappit. Can I just ask - is there anyone here who's not a Yapper?' There were headshakes and grunts and mumbles from the crowd but no hands went up. 'Right, so everyone here is on Yappit, and I know that many of you read the Yaps that I post, the stories, the jokes, the comments and riddles about life.'

Nods and muttering agreement from the crowd. 'No doubt you've got your favourites. The ones you pass onto others, the ones you find particularly funny or provocative. There are probably some that pass you by - not everyone gets everything.'

Some knowing laughter from the crowd.

'However, I've got a surprise for you, I'm not just the most popular Yapper.' He faltered for a second, glanced around, and licked his lips. 'Sooner or later I knew the news would break, so I thought I'd bring it myself to the town that I love.' He cleared his throat. 'I'm not just the top Yapper,' he said, 'I own the whole network. I designed it, financed it, dreamt the whole thing up. This thing you're all part of is owned by me. I monitor it all, without me you couldn't Yap. And I could close it down tomorrow. Why am I telling you all this? Because I want you to get the best from it. I want more interaction with you, I want to improve the way Yappit works. But I need your

114

help. I need you to stay locked in to the network and see where we all go in the next few years. We need to make changes, to grow and develop, which may be demanding, difficult even, but I don't want you to give up. I need you. If you leave Yappit you lose all the benefits, if you stay, who knows how we'll develop and where you'll end up? Yappit will change the way you see your world. But it's up to you? Who's with me?'

The Bit Where Dave Explains How to Be Fruitful...

Bearing fruit is probably easiest if you're an apple tree. It's practically impossible if you're a table. What is also certain is this, apple trees can't produce grapes and grapevines can't produce watermelons. Magicians can produce anything from anywhere, but a rabbit from a hat is not going to solve the world's problems.

The kind of fruit that will solve the world's problems includes love, joy, peace, patience, goodness, kindness and pomegranates. But you can probably do it without the pomegranates. This kind of fruit can't be bought or sold, even on eBay. It can only be nurtured in the soil of life. This is also a problem because you can't buy the soil of life in a big plastic sack from a garden centre. You can buy slug pellets and rat traps but they're unlikely to be useful when you want to make the world a better place. Unless your world is overrun with slugs and rats, which is possible. Or maybe it just feels like that.

The good news is the fruit of love is free. You don't need money or a credit card, the bad news is there are no Nectar points. A man in a film once said, 'If you ask for patience d'you think God gives you patience, or does he give you opportunities to be patient?' The man was playing God, which of course we all do from time to time. But he had a point. If we ask God for kindness maybe he gives us times when we can be kind. If we ask for more happiness he might give us a joke book. If we ask for a huge mountain of chocolate he'll probably just say no.

Fruit of course can go rotten. At any point in time two thirds of the world's fridges contain at least one piece of fruit that's about to turn nuclear. Ripe fruit falls off the tree, it's as if the tree is saying, 'Take this lot away will you, it's good to go.' If no one responds the tree gets huffy and the fruit gets all rotten. Likewise, any fruit you bear is only really good if other people help themselves to it. If you want proof - look at any comedian. Most funny people are miserable as sin, but they can have an audience rolling in the aisles. Humour is their fruit and we are the sad people that pick it.

Apple trees take time out in the winter. They don't go off to Jamaica or anything, they just shut down and sulk for a while. And who can blame them with the British winters? If you want to stop bearing fruit for a while it's possible to unplug yourself from the soil of life. But don't hang about out there too long or bits of you might just curl up, turn brown and furry, and die. And then the only thing left to do is get all maggoty and turn into mulch.

John 15 vv 1-4

¹ 'I am the true vine, and my Father is the gardener. ² He cuts off every branch that doesn't produce fruit, and he prunes the branches that do bear fruit so they will produce even more. ³ You have already been pruned for greater fruitfulness by the message I have given you. ⁴ Remain in me, and I will remain in you. For a branch cannot produce fruit if it is severed from the vine, and you cannot be fruitful apart from me.'

The Serious Bit

In the book of Jeremiah there is a promise. One day a branch will sit on the king's throne and run the place properly. Now obviously we're not talking about a bit of gnarled wood here. The branch is itself a metaphor for a king. A Messiah who will bring in a new age of freedom, peace and justice. And Jesus messes with that image. He just can't seem to help himself sometimes.

'I am the vine,' he says, 'and you are the branches.' This turns everything on its head. Israel was supposed to be the vine bringing fruit to the world and the king was the branch. Nope, Jesus wants to be the vine, he'll be the true Israelite who will do the job of serving the world, and the rest of us, we get to be the branches.

When someone asked Jesus one day who was their neighbour, he didn't answer the question. Instead he told a story which said,

'Go and be a neighbour' - get involved. When a woman at a well asked him for some life-giving water, he said, 'You can certainly have some but then you become a carrier, you can bring life-giving water to others too. You can get involved.'

The people wanted a 'branch' to come and save them from their problems. Jesus pulled the rug from under them by saying, 'I'll be the vine - you be the branch – you get involved with saving the world from its problems.'

Yikes, I don't want to get involved. Don't you understand, Jesus, I'm just not very good at being a branch. I'm close to breaking point sometimes. I just want to go to church and feel better about myself. Nope says Jesus. There's more to it.

Want to try?

?   ?   ?   ?

The Split
(The Workers in the Vineyard)

Dave's Version

The getaway was astonishing. No one would have given the two bungling thieves much chance of success after they had robbed the food store. The haul wasn't huge, approximately £2000, but they needed the cash. The problem was, they were not very adept at stealing. As they sped out of the shop and down the busy high street they collided with almost everybody else coming the other way. They dropped their bags, their guns, their masks and most importantly the money. A passing group of kids took pity on them and helped them pick everything up, then they ran on with them down the street as they heard the sound of the police coming. The gang, now fifteen of them, slipped off the high street and down a side ally. Big problem. It wasn't a neat getaway, it was a dead-end. They huddled in the gloom by the huge brick wall at the far end listening to the sound of the police closing in. Then they heard another sound - the sound of tapping. It wasn't a leaking pipe, it was a girl knocking on a nearby window in the building next to them in the alley. One of the gang

recognised her, she was an old friend. They hadn't seen each other in years. She realised their plight and opened the window to let them in. Gratefully the gang bundled inside.

It was a library. The gang stared horrified and promptly dropped their guns, money, bags and masks all over again as silent faces looked up and studied them, with bemused and perplexed expressions. The girl and her five friends helped them pick it all up and they then ran very obviously through the building. The gang of twenty-one spilled out onto the pavement, being shushed fiercely as they went. The police, who were just re-emerging from the alley, promptly spotted them. They were caught.

Or so they thought. There was the sound of a blaring horn and a double-decker bus pulled up next to them. The doors opened and the driver called to them. He was an old friend, an ex-vicar who'd changed jobs. They jumped on board, the bus pulling away just in time as the police threw themselves at the escaping gang. The bus shot down the high street and away from the danger. But the passengers were not happy. The gang was now twenty-one strong and the sudden invasion of bodies upset a lot of the regular travellers. Some of them started to get up and threaten the crooks. The driver saw trouble coming and pulled over again. He let the gang off and jumped off with them, realising he was now implicated too. They hurried on only to run smack into a band of buskers doing a reggae version of Bohemian Rhapsody. The gang hit them so hard everything went flying. Keyboard, amps, guitars, xylophone, harpsichord and musicians. The band were furious till they took a close look at the gang and realised they were all mates. They grabbed the guns, cash, bags and masks which had been dropped again in the collision and led the gang to a nearby house. It belonged to the grandparents of the lead singer. And there the gang hid until the police had given up the chase.

That evening they counted the cash and decided to split it. Then they counted the gang. Two grandparents, three neighbours who regularly dropped by to watch old recordings of *Songs of Praise*, eight band members, an ex-vicar bus driver, the librarian and her five friends, thirteen kids from the street and two thieves.

They had just under £2000, and an argument about who should get paid.

Thief One: What are you doing, Pete?

Thief Two: We agreed right? We'd split it.

Thief One: Yea. Two ways. We don't owe this lot anything.

Thief Two: John, we wouldn't be standing here with any money at all if it wasn't for her... and him... and him...and them... and them and her...

Thief One: Yea but <u>we</u> did the job.

Thief Two: We all did the job. You gonna tell me I'm stupid for paying them for what they did?

Thief One: No. All right, just give 'em a little bit.

Thief Two: No, they're in the gang now.

Thief One: We don't have a gang.

Thief Two: Yea we do, John. The moment they stopped to help us they joined. We get caught – they get caught. That's the deal. We're all equal. We all get the same reward. It doesn't matter when we joined the gang. We all get paid.

The Bit Where Dave Explains About Just Desserts...

Working out what we deserve is much easier now we have a minimum wage. We now know that 1085.81 euros is the answer. This is of course not per minute but per month before deduction of income tax and social security contributions and not adjusted for inflation. And we all suffer from inflation. Our egos tend to suffer the most, getting over-inflated just when there is the wrong person nearby with a pin the size of the Eiffel Tower to lance and deflate that particular occurrence.

Some people do earn 1085.81 euros per minute, and they often work on the 157th floor in a large banking corporation. They probably don't read this parable on a regular basis. Or if they do it's only so they can have a good laugh. The idea that we should all get one euro per day irrespective of how many hours we put in and how inflated our egos are seems daft to them. They are, after all, very important people.

Thinking you are very important and everyone else is not quite so important is the best road to be on if you want to imagine that you deserve just that little bit more than other people. This is clearly where the man from Nazareth went so wrong. As the Messiah of the world and the creator of pretty much everything, he deserved a lot more than a criminal's death. You don't need to be rocket scientists to work out that the Creator of the Universe should get a little bit more than a criminal's minimum wage. But what can you expect when you go round making up naïve stories about everybody getting the same reward.

The Bible says that the wages of sin is death. In other words, a criminal's minimum wage. Nobody wants to think they are on the fast track to that, but many people do think that their wages are worse. Garages used to give away free gifts with a gallon of petrol. Unfortunately we no longer buy gallons of fuel which may be why we no longer get free gifts. Even if those free gifts were just chipped glasses it's disappointing.

The free gift we can all still claim is full eternal life, which is not to be sneezed at. Especially as you don't have to buy a litre of petrol, which lets' face it, costs the earth these days. Free life is available without even crossing a Tesco's forecourt. You can get it anywhere you like, as long as you don't mind it being a free gift available to everyone. Including criminals and bankers.

Matthew 20 vv 1-15

1 "For the Kingdom of Heaven is like the owner of an estate who went out early one morning to hire workers for his vineyard. 2 He agreed to pay the normal daily wage and sent them out to work.
3 "At nine o'clock in the morning he was passing through the marketplace and saw some people standing around doing nothing.
4 So he hired them, telling them he would pay them whatever was right at the end of the day. 5 At noon and again around three o'clock he did the same thing. 6 At five o'clock that evening he was in town again and saw some more people standing around. He asked them, 'Why haven't you been working today?'
7 "They replied, 'Because no one hired us.'"
The owner of the estate told them, 'then go on out and join the others in my vineyard.'
8 "That evening he told the foreman to call the workers in and pay them, beginning with the last workers first. 9 When those hired at five o'clock were paid, each received a full day's wage. 10 When those hired earlier came to get their pay, they assumed they would receive more. But they, too, were paid a day's wage.
11 When they received their pay, they protested, 12 'Those people worked only one hour, and yet you've paid them just as much as you paid us who worked all day in the scorching heat.'
13 "He answered one of them, 'Friend, I haven't been unfair! Didn't you agree to work all day for the usual wage? 14 Take it and go. I wanted to pay this last worker the same as you. 15 Is it against the law for me to do what I want with my money? Should you be angry because I am kind?'"

The Serious Bit

God can sometimes seem naïve, don't you think? I mean, no workforce on earth would put up with this outcome. There would be an outcry. Strikes. Some have sweated for twelve hours, some have sweated... not much really. Some have done an average day's work. I guess Jesus knows that money is a powerful tool when it comes to parables. Some will sneer, some will laugh, some will be amazed, some will think – if only, if only. But one thing's for sure - money will get a response.

I am currently listening to a debate on radio about whether or not women should be paid the same as men. Apparently research shows that they are generally paid less. One male caller said that other people have no moral right to know what he earns. This parable would not go down well, would it? Especially as these folks in the story clearly do know what they are all getting and don't like it.

People sometimes say that religion and politics should never mix, this may be because of the money issue. We should keep our wallets and our prayer books in different pockets. Money after all, makes the world go round, why muddy the waters with complicated theological issues? And of course – this is a metaphor, it's not really about how to go about hiring workers.

Theologian Tom Wright points out that there is an interesting comment towards the end of this parable. The last group to get hired claim that they have been hanging around waiting for work all day, but nobody hired them. These are the losers, the unpopular ones. These are the people who never get picked for the football team, never got spotted in a crowd, never get mistaken for part of the in-crowd. Jesus hires them. He takes a risk. God goes into the marketplace looking for those that others ignore.

Just before Jesus told this story a close friend had asked him, 'What's in it for us? What are we going to get out of following you?' Ever ask that question? I do. Jesus's reply is both encouraging and frustrating. You'll get what everyone will get. So good news then... and bad. The same reward. God is kind and generous to all of us. This is not about getting what you can from the creator, this is about an offer made freely *by* the creator. He calls the shots, not us.

It's easy to take the generous offer from God and manipulate it to our own ends. I once heard a TV evangelist encourage people to give because Jesus promised that you would get a hundredfold in return. So invest a pound with Reverend Smarmy Exploiter and you're sure to get a hundred back. Forgive the forthcoming expletive but... that's crap. It doesn't work like that.

How are your wages?

?   ?   ?   ?

Grumpy Old Men
(The Pharisee and the Tax Collector)

Dave's Version

Two men went to the Temple to pray. One was a grumpy old Pharisee, and the other was a grumpy old tax collector. The grumpy old Pharisee stood by himself and prayed this prayer:

'I thank you, God, that I am not a sinner like everyone else, especially like that tax collector over there! For I never cheat, I don't sin, I don't commit adultery, I fast twice a week, and I give you a tenth of my income.'

But the grumpy old tax collector stood at a distance, beat on his chest in sorrow and dared not even lift his eyes to heaven as he prayed:

'Oh Lord, thank you that we're not like the younger generation. We're not greedy or dishonest, we don't play loud music, or wear outrageous clothes. And we respect our elders.'

Pharisee: Yes Lord, it's all changed hasn't it. I remember when you could buy a new suit, 3 pairs of shoes and a bag of chips all for sixpence.

Tax C: Yes Lord, it's all gone so wrong, hasn't it. Belly button rings, tattoos, bleached hair...

Pharisee: Not to mention them mobile smartphones.

Tax C: Huh - dumb phones more like. Don't get me started on those. Those annoying little Beyoncé ring tones, and people on trains always talking loudly. Hello dear I'll be home in three hours... Hello dear I'll be home in two hours... Hello dear I'll be home in one hour... Hello dear, I can see you out on the station... SHUT UP! We'll have them in church soon.

Pharisee: Church! Don't get me started on church. We used to have choir robes and lovely hymns. Do you remember?

Tax C: Oh aye – (sings) Jesus loves me, this I know, for the Bible tells me so er... la, la, la la, la la la...

Pharisee: Ah, they don't write words like that no more.

Tax C: We didn't need these bongo drums and flag waving – buxom ladies prancing around like young adolescents and them worship leaders in crop tops and baggy jeans.

Pharisee: Jeans, don't get me started on jeans, in my day if you came to church in jeans you'd be burnt at the stake for being a witch. Moses didn't wear jeans did he? And you wouldn't wear jeans, would ya, Levi?

Tax C: No and Jesus didn't play a guitar. Or use Powerpoint!

Pharisee: Powerpoint! Don't get me started on Powerpoint? Letters swirling around making you feel sea sick, pictures of your holiday snaps behind the hymns and choruses...

Tax C: Choruses! Don't get me started on choruses. 'I really really just really just love you Lord' sung 27 times.

Pharisee: It can't be right. If God had wanted things to change – he'd have given us imaginations!

Tax C: Come on let's go and watch Songs of Praise.

Pharisee: Songs of Praise, don't get me started on that... I remember when it was in black and white...

And Jesus said, 'I tell you the truth, both grumpy old sinners went home, unaware that they'd been forgiven.'

A Few More Bits About How to Judge People...

Chr: I look down on him because he is agnostic.

Agn: I look up to him because he is a Christian. But I look down on him because he is an atheist.

Ath: I know my place.

Chr: I get a feeling of superiority over him because I have it all worked out.

Agn: I get a feeling of inferiority from him because I'm not sure, but a feeling of superiority over him.

Ath: I get a pain in the back of my neck.

?   ?   ?   ?

1: I look down on him because I am charismatic and I go to New Wine.

2: I look down on him because I am high church and I enjoy a lot of new wine.

3: I am Methodist. We have Ribena.

?   ?   ?   ?

4:     I look down on him because he is a catholic.
5:     I look down on him because he is a protestant.
God: I look down on all of them and wonder why they can't all just get along.

Luke 18 vv 9-14

[9] Then Jesus told this story to some who had great self-confidence and scorned everyone else: [10] "Two men went to the Temple to pray. One was a Pharisee, and the other was a dishonest tax collector. [11] The proud Pharisee stood by himself and prayed this prayer: 'I thank you, God, that I am not a sinner like everyone else, especially like that tax collector over there! For I never cheat, I don't sin, I don't commit adultery, [12] I fast twice a week, and I give you a tenth of my income.' [13] "But the tax collector stood at a distance and dared not even lift his eyes to heaven as he prayed. Instead, he beat his chest in sorrow, saying, 'O God, be merciful to me, for I am a sinner.' [14] I tell you, this sinner, not the Pharisee, returned home justified before God. For the proud will be humbled, but the humble will be honoured."

The Serious Bit

Looking down on others is easier if you're taller. It's not easy for the seven dwarves to look down on the giant at the top of Jack's beanstalk. But John Cleese has every right to look down on Ronnie Corbett and proved it in that satirical sketch. It was impossible for David to look down on Goliath. Until he produced a sling and brought the big man down to size a bit.

I like to think I don't judge others. I'm proud of that fact and I'm annoyed with all those people who do judge others. Why can't they just be a little more humble? Why is it so difficult to get along, can't we just be a little more accepting and stop measuring ourselves against all those losers?

One day all those 'Pharisees' will get what they deserve. And it'll be about time too.
I don't look down on them though. I'd never do that.

?   ?   ?   ?

Mack and the Knife
(The Hidden Treasure and The Pearl)

Dave's Version

When Mack Durban was offered three times the asking price for one of his fields he should have suspected something. But Mack was keen to sell, and when Denise Brown turned up with a fistful of notes he couldn't resist her offer. He took the money and handed over ownership of the land, only to watch her produce a spade from the boot of her 4x4 and promptly start digging a hole. It turned out Denise was an avid treasure hunter and she'd discovered a rare artefact just that morning. The Cordoban Dagger is a thousand years old and priceless; once thought lost forever it had somehow washed up in Mack's back garden.
'A worthwhile investment,' she said as she showed him the find.

In the end though Mack wasn't complaining. He'd spotted a rare stamp for sale in a collection in a local antique shop. The asking price for the complete set was high, but nothing compared to the value of the unused Indian Scinde Dawk nestled in the heart of the collection. Mack took every penny he'd got from the field and immediately went down to Antique Kingdom and put it all on the counter in exchange for the collection. The owner saw him coming and hiked the price up but Mack barely noticed, it was still only a fraction of the value of the one stamp he was looking for.

Three months later as Denise was showing the dagger to a couple of friends one of them noticed what she had missed. On the back, etched in the precious metal, there was a name. Hernan Luis Gomez. This meant nothing to her friends but Denise knew. This piece was part of a unique collection. There was more treasure out there, more work to be done. Mack didn't take three months, he spotted the tiny coded map reference on the back of the Scinde Dawk almost immediately. It would take a while to work it out, but he would get there, and then who knows where the trail might lead.

The Bit Where Dave Explains How to Find Treasure...

There are places to look for treasure, like the attic or the cellar or a big ship at the bottom of the ocean, or a desert island that came with a map saying 'Blackbeard was here'. There are other places that it's best not to look. Like down the back of the sofa, under the carpet or up your own nose. You will find things and there will be surprises, but it's unlikely that you'll sell everything else you have to keep hold of them.

Many people collect things, like stamps, or husbands, or their children from school, or tropical diseases. Some people use metal detectors and walk across fields like policeman searching for that vital clue to prove that the butler done it. Half the world's treasures are concealed just below the surface of most of the farms in Norfolk, Aztec gold, Incan jewellery and Roman ruins all got left behind here when the Vikings left.

The man from Nazareth didn't have much treasure himself. He once found a coin in a fish's mouth but that went on his taxes which were extortionate. The Romans made everyone pay VAT without ever giving them any value whatsoever.

The best treasure is not a long-forgotten second stab at the Mona Lisa that no one realised Leonardo had done on a rainy Monday morning one week. The really valuable stuff includes things that no one can steal from you or borrow and not return or persuade you to sell on eBay. This is the kind of treasure that will last forever. Even longer than the DFS sale or the turkey leftovers at Christmas. No one can place a value on it so there's not much point taking it along to *Cash in the Attic* or *The Antiques Roadshow* and queuing for hours behind that man with the hat and the whip and the Holy Grail.

In fact, you already have the Holy Grail if you've found this treasure, and it won't fall down a crack in the ground when an earthquake hits the cave you happen to be standing in. Steven Spielberg will probably never make a movie about it, but by the same token, you can never lose it and nothing can steal it away.

The Serious Bit

One of the things I have said many times about these two parables is that they are not the same. The first likens the kingdom of God to some treasure found by a man, something precious worth selling everything for. But the second likens the kingdom of God to *a man looking for precious pearls*. In this story the pearl represents something else, the kingdom is represented by the man looking for pearls. We are not the only ones searching - the kingdom of God is out searching too, looking for us, and when it finds us it will give everything to get us. This is unexpected and yet once again, it's only really a description of what Jesus is up to. The kingdom of God is not just about good things we can get into our lives, but it's a man who's come looking, a man who knows what he's looking for. A man who will literally give up his whole life to find us and buy us.

The old prophet Jeremiah once brought a message from God which said 'If you look for me in earnest, you will find me when you seek me. I will be found by you.'
It's as if God is hiding, waiting for us to come looking. Playing a game of divine/human hide and seek. There is an old saying - a man chases a woman till she catches him. In other words we look for something until it finds us. Jesus said on one occasion, 'Keep asking, looking and knocking on those doors.' Keep searching for God till he finds you.

There is something inherent about the faith that demands we

never call off the search. Even when we have 'been converted', found the treasure if you like, there is plenty more to discover. It's as if the treasure chest contains some gold and a key to another chest, buried somewhere else. Some more treasure which also contains another key, which contains another key, which contains another one...

The hunt goes on forever.

?   ?   ?   ?

Aldemia's Dark Secret
(The Rich Fool)

Dave's Version

Aldemia confessed its dark secret to the world last night. It has a fruitcake mountain. Aldemia has long been the producer of fine grapes and nuts and sugar. These have proved to be most useful in the fruitcake production market. And until recently fruitcake was the big Aldemian export. However, the product proved so marketable that the stock became dangerously low five years ago, so the minister for food Douglas Dyad, or 'dieting Douglas' as he is known here, placed a ban on exports. This would have been a highly commendable step but for the fact that DD is known to be rather partial to Aldemia's finest, and he has adamantly refused to lift the ban since.

So now the country has hundreds of barns chock full of fermenting cakes and puddings. Charities have called for the government to give away the ridiculously massive stockpile, claiming that the country is on the verge of a catastrophic culinary disaster. If the barns get infested with rats the entire stock will be ruined and the rodent population could go through the roof. Dieting Douglas is currently away and unavailable for comment but rumours abound regarding the protest group the FFA, Free Fruit for Aldemia, some claiming that the group are planning a large-scale barn invasion to free the incarcerated food.

The Bit Where Dave Explains What to Do with Things...

Getting addicted to something is quite easy. Just do it enough times and blam! you're in. Sadly this only seems to work though with the expensive and unhelpful things in life. Do the washing up ten times a day and you're unlikely to crave *Fairy Liquid* and greasy plates. Consume twelve bars of chocolate and/or a hundred cigarettes before elevenses, and you may well be leaning over a toilet by lunch, but after you've mopped up and tucked into a diced carrot sandwich, you may well then find a renewed craving for cocoa powder and nicotine. Shopping is addictive too of course. Buy a pint of milk and before too long you're bound to need another. Bread also has this terrible stigma attached to it. Many a celebrity has been caught on camera lurking by the crumpets and croissants in Morrisons.

We all need things. Things make us feel worthwhile. Brand new things are shiny and come into our lives smelling all leathery, well new shoes do anyway. If new cream cakes come in smelling like that I'd give them a wide berth. Likewise if you're shoes come in smelling of cream and jam you might get a few funny looks. It's easy to fall in love with things, they don't clog up the sink with matted hair, or refuse to change the loo roll, or leave their breakfast things on your side of the bed. Things can also be replaced without a lot of fuss and the involvement of expensive lawyers.

Sharing can be difficult, especially if you have barns full of stuff. The more barns you have the more barn door keys you have to lose. When you reach the point when your barn is full you have a choice. You can either do the easy thing of just throwing a party and/or soup kitchen thereby giving away the surplus, or you can organise the builders, dress up as the Amish, have a barn-raising and get another set of keys cut. Bearing in mind that on average five sets of keys are lost every twenty-seven seconds, bringing another set of keys into the world may not be the best idea.

People are different from things. They have minds of their own which is a problem because their mind is clearly not yours and they refuse to change it. Loving people takes a lot of sweat, toil, patience and generosity. Buying other people things is useful because it makes them feel good. It can make you feel good too, until that cold grey winter's morning when you find yourself poring over the Mastercard bill. It has been said that it's better to give than to receive. Certainly this is true of a thick ear or a bruised shin, though you may get back more than you gave. This is also true concerning the things we are tempted to love. If we give these to the people we are tempted to love then we may get back more than we gave.

As long as the gifts don't smell leathery when they should smell of cream and jam and vice versa.

Luke 12 vv 13-21

¹³ Then someone called from the crowd, "Teacher, please tell my brother to divide our father's estate with me."
¹⁴ Jesus replied, "Friend, who made me a judge over you to decide such things as that?" ¹⁵ Then he said, "Beware! Don't be greedy for what you don't have. Real life is not measured by how much we own."
¹⁶ And he gave an illustration: "A rich man had a fertile farm that produced fine crops. ¹⁷ In fact, his barns were full to overflowing. ¹⁸ So he said, 'I know! I'll tear down my barns and build bigger ones. Then I'll have room enough to store everything. ¹⁹ And I'll sit back and say to myself, my friend, you have enough stored away for years to come. Now take it easy! Eat, drink, and be merry!'
²⁰ "But God said to him, 'You fool! You will die this very night. Then who will get it all?'
²¹ "Yes, a person is a fool to store up earthly wealth but not have a rich relationship with God."

The Serious Bit

There is a moment in the film *Bobby* when Jack turns to his wife Samantha and, after removing her designer shoes says, 'Somewhere between our things and our stuff is us.'
This is a mantra for those of us who live in the west. Even after a credit crunch and with a recession going on we are still amongst the most wealthy in the world. So many people have so much less.

This parable is a bit of history retold. There is this rich fool in the Old Testament called Nabal. His name means stupid and he lives up to it. One day when the soon-to-be king David shows up looking for help, Nabal refuses to share what he has. This brings out the worst in both Nabal and David, but thankfully, not Nabal's clever wife Abigail. She sees an opportunity and dives in with all her wit and cunning. David, angry and embarrassed by Nabal's snub vows to 'get his own back' and begins to plan for revenge, but at the last moment Abigail arrives with loads of pressies and an apology. She tells David he will regret killing her husband. One day he will be a great king and he really doesn't want stupid Nabal's blood on his hands forever haunting him. She bows, smiles and puts in a request as she leaves, 'Remember me when you get your kingdom.'

Abigail is a wise woman. David, thankfully, tucks his pride in his back pocket. Nabal has a heart attack when he finds out what's been going on. The rich fool refuses to share the abundance he has and dies. Abigail's smile was not wasted - David does remember her - and having lost one husband she finds herself with another one. One day soon she will be a queen. You could call it the parable of the wise and foolish married couple.

I used to think that all Jesus's parables were about how to get into heaven. Now it seems that most of them are about how we operate on earth. What will we do with our stuff? Will we let it control us?
Somewhere between Jack and Samantha, and Abigail and Nabal, and Jesus and the rich fool...

is us.

?   ?   ?   ?

The Black Box
(In My Father's House)

Dave's Version

The boy is nervous, he's young
and scared. He has no idea
how she will react and he
fingers the black box anxiously.
Everything rests on this, the
future will never be the same
whichever way this goes.
Here she comes now and his
heart misses a beat, he feels
like he's loved her forever.
She's the most beautiful girl
he's ever seen, he'd walk
through fire for her, he'd take a
bullet.
He picks at the flecks of paint
under his nails.

She's human of course, she's
no goddess, he's not stupid.
She annoys him with her
stupid jokes and her taste in
music and the way she
always has to taste everything
on his plate.

She's tired, distracted, had a
hard day, the kids were
playing up, it's still only halfway
through the term but
everyone's frazzled already.
He lets her talk, tries hard not
to quick-fix all her problems.
She hates it when he does
that. Eventually she falls quiet,
sips her wine, gives him a
quiet smile.
'I've got something to ask you,'
he says.

She frowns.
'Don't worry,' he says, 'it's not
money, I got paid.'
'It's not your mate John again,
is it?' she says. 'I can't stand
another few days of him. His
roll-ups and disgusting finger
nails.'
He laughs and shakes his
head. 'It's not John.' He fishes
in his pocket, pulls out the little
black box. He says nothing,
opens it, places it on the table.
She stares at it.
'What's that?' she says.
'It's a key,' he says.
'I can see that. Why?'
'My dad's flat. He's given it to
me, I've been redecorating it.
Getting it ready.'
'For what?'
Silence, a pause, he clears his
throat.
'For you.'
He places a second black box
on the table. She reaches out
and opens it, says nothing.
'I've been working hard,
preparing the place for us,
getting a new life ready. It's
nearly done, a few more days
and the job'll be finished.
What do you say? Please say
yes?'
She stares at the two boxes.
The key, then the ring, then
back to the key. This will
change everything.

The Bit Where Dave Explains About Weddings...

I'm not sure if the man from Nazareth was very tidy. It all depends
on whether you can picture his mother Mary saying, 'Come on Jesus,
get that first century Lego put away, we've got the wise men popping
round to see how you've grown. I need your help to sort things out,
see if we can track down that bit of gold they gave us.'
He *was* a builder and a carpenter though, so when he said 'I'm going to
prepare a room for you' he may not have had a hoover and a duster in
mind, but he could have been all set to construct something.

Nowadays the groom's preparation for marriage includes bending
down on one knee, buying a ring and choosing a best man who won't
embarrass him too much. Not necessarily in that order. Re the best
man it's probably best to pick a friend you haven't known for too
long, someone who knows very little about your dark past, e.g.
someone who happens to be passing by when you're having the stag
do. Anyone who stops long enough to free you from the lamppost is
probably a good candidate.

When the man from Nazareth was around it was the groom's job to
get a whole new place constructed. So the stag do probably resembled
a tea break on a building site; there may not have been much time
for go-karting, paintballing or grouse shooting. There might have
been a bit of off-roading when scavenging for building materials and
dodging Roman hit-squads, but that was about it. Most of the parties
back then were thrown by Caesars, sinners and tax collectors.
Caesars were always getting married, usually to their closest relative.

Weddings back then went on for a week, and included the
consummation, when all the guests would hang around nearby. This
was a little frustrating if you'd seen the size of the vol-au-vents and
were desperate to get stuck in. The whole village pitched up so you
got quite an audience.

Why all this talk about grooms and weddings? Well, the main thing
to remember here is that the man from Nazareth often pictured
himself as a bridegroom; it was a regular image for him, a metaphor
that runs through the whole of the good book. And when he talked of
preparing a room he was in mid-conversation with Peter, a good
friend who, had Jesus ever married, might well have been his best
man. In this particular conversation Peter's just had some very bad
news, so he's a man in dire need of some encouragement. When
you've just been warned that you're about to make the most serious

mistake you'll ever make, then it's worth knowing that there's a second chance waiting round the corner.

John 13 v 36 – 14 v 4

[36]Simon Peter said, "Lord, where are you going?"

And Jesus replied, "You can't go with me now, but you will follow me later."

[37] "But why can't I come now, Lord?" he asked. "I am ready to die for you."

[38]Jesus answered, "Die for me? No, before the rooster crows tomorrow morning, you will deny three times that you even know me. [1] Don't be troubled. You trust God, now trust in me. [2] There are many rooms in my Father's home, and I am going to prepare a place for you. If this were not so, I would tell you plainly. [3]When everything is ready, I will come and get you, so that you will always be with me where I am. [4]And you know where I am going and how to get there."

The Serious Bit

I decided to finish with this parable for a couple of reasons. Firstly a lot of people may not realise that it is a parable, and secondly because it's a great example of why we need to read the Bible in context.

The reply Jesus makes about going to prepare a place for us in his father's house is widely accepted as being a reference to Jesus ascending to heaven and getting a place ready for us there. But that isn't what the disciples would have understood. When Jesus first said these things he didn't announce that this statement would make up the first couple of verses in chapter 13 of the best-selling book John would write soon. This comment follows on logically in the conversation he is having with one of his closest friends. So what has just happened?

He has just told Peter that the poor guy is about to betray him, about to let himself and the others down badly. This is devastating news but Jesus follows it up with another prophecy, and encourages Peter to not be worried about this terrible betrayal because he is about to go and do something profound. And now comes the little parable, and once again Jesus is drawing on the image of himself as the bridegroom, or the wannabe bridegroom. In Peter's day when a man was to marry his bride he would go to the family home and ask his father for a room in or near where the family lived, sometimes extra rooms were built on the side of the dad's house, or nearby in a small complex as part of the home community.

So Jesus suddenly seems to switch here from warning Peter about betrayal to talking about marriage.
'Don't worry,' he says, 'my father has a big house. I'm going to get a room ready for you, and though I'm going away (to die) I'll come back soon (be resurrected) and then I will have done the work required to prepare a new life for you.' In the same way that a groom prepared a new beginning for his bride, Jesus's sacrifice is preparing a new start for Peter. And that's why Peter does not need to worry. Because, in spite of his upcoming failure, Jesus already has it in hand, not just Peter's but everyone's failure is about to be redeemed by Jesus's death and resurrection.

Of course Jesus's death is about preparing a place for us in God's kingdom too, but in this context Jesus is encouraging his friend about a new start in this life. A new beginning which means Jesus is present with us wherever we go.
'You'll make mistakes,' he says to Peter and to us, 'but I'm working on a new life for you, a new relationship, a new way of being, a new chance to start again. Watch closely, the next three days will change everything.'

Those words of encouragement stand for all time.

?   ?   ?   ?

Bonus Extra:

A few yarns of my own making…

NIL
by
MOUTH

Dispensing Reality
Without Spoonfeeding It

"It is most tempting to want to impress hope upon
others by delivering truth on a plate.
There are other ways of communicating."

A parable communicates with the inner self.
It is a tool for saying hard things, or mysterious things
in a pleasant, often entertaining way.
Advertisers employ it regularly. The church less so.

The Bible relies heavily upon the power of story. When
considering parables we often think of Jesus's stories,
but the Old Testament is full of symbolic tales and
imagery. For example, the psalms regularly use the
word '*like*':
**"We have escaped _like_
a bird from a hunter's trap..."** (Psalm 124 v 7)

In an age when we are surrounded and bombarded
with rhetoric (which we know instinctively will come to
nothing) stories and parables make a welcome
and refreshing change.

Of course, the problem with a parable is that it leaves
the story teller open to misinterpretation, but it is that
same vulnerability which invites discussion and
encourages others to draw near and discover more.

I have offered no explanation
with each of these stories,
you may well discover pearls
of your own hidden in them...

How can we sum up the value of that which is priceless? It's like a woman who bought an instant lottery ticket in a newsagents, and found she'd won the £50,000 prize. What does she do? She's so excited she dances down the street, leaps into the air and accidentally flings the ticket into a newly laid cement path, belonging to the house just next to the shop. Unable to pull it out and retrieve it she returns home, sells her flat, goes back and buys the house where she dropped the ticket. Then she hires a builder to break up the cement path so she can get hold of the ticket again and claim the prize.

Or it's like a man who won the £10 million Jackpot, but then couldn't find his ticket. He turned his house upside-down, carried all his furniture outside, turned out his wardrobes, x-rayed his pets, interrogated his relatives. When he finally found the ticket, in the place he'd put it for safekeeping, he carried it everywhere he went. He kept it sealed inside a plastic wallet, which was chained to his wrist with his grandfather's gold watch chain. He kept himself awake drinking black coffee and playing loud music. He avoided any other distractions, just in case he should take his eyes off the ticket again and lose his prize. When he finally came to claim his money - he handed over the ticket, took the cash and went straight out to throw the biggest party he could possibly afford...

How should we describe what is indescribable... it's like standing outside a cupboard, the door is plain, boring, of little obvious interest. But on opening the cupboard all kinds of treasure may be discovered. Wonderful, precious, dangerous, intriguing items fill the place. Jewels drip from the shelves, gilt-edged books sag open - revealing untold mystery and wisdom. Rich dark secrets drape from the ceiling. But how may this treasure be discovered, if we only stand on the outside of the cupboard, gazing from afar at a rather plain, wooden door?

The kingdom is rather like a Magic Eye Picture - you look at it for a long time and can make no sense of it. It seems strange, distant, frustrating and annoying. You feel you're an outsider, deprived and frustrated by those already in the know. They cannot make you see it for yourself, though they may try to push you into it. Then one day - it clicks. The view changes, the vision alters, and your eyes adjust to the new world before them. The two-dimensional takes on new shape, images leap out at you, the objects move before your gaze, and suddenly you are inside - no longer squinting from a distance, but revelling in this amazing new experience. And though it may not always happen easily, you will always be part of this new kingdom of colour, beauty, light and shade - no longer an outsider, but understanding that which was only a blurred enigma before...

A group of people arrived in Chocolate World. The visit was unplanned, none of them had expected to drop in so soon, but their host was most welcoming. There were many departments in Chocolate World, he informed them, all tastes catered for - the liqueur filled, the rich dark, the solid slabs, the soft centres; places for those who only ate pure chocolate, and places for those who welcomed any kind of sweet. Some were surprised at this last group being present (this was Chocolate World, after all) but they were all duly ushered off to their respective rooms. One group remained, however, they didn't know about liqueurs, truffles, or soft centres - they just loved chocolate. The host smiled, "So do I." he said, and he gave them complete freedom of the place...

Once there was a farmer who went out to sow his crops. He gathered together the bags of seed, bought in extra fertiliser and set to work. He threw open all the windows of the farmhouse and called out enthusiastically to the acres of fertile fields that lay expectantly before him. He beckoned to them, waved the sacks of fertiliser, offered them the bags of seed and demonstrated how important it was for the crops to be sown. But the fields wouldn't budge. Day after day the farmer went to the front door and waited, but the land never came any closer. Occasionally he resorted to throwing large handfuls of the seed out of the bedroom windows, but it only fell on the path and was scooped up by the wind and the birds. Come harvest time his barns were still empty and he sadly wondered why the fields were so stubborn, and the land was so bare...

144

Once there was a man and woman who fell in love. They married and lived happily together until the wife began seeing another man. The wife was very beautiful, and it wasn't long before they embarked on a passionate affair and conducted this in secret for several months. Eventually the inevitable happened, the husband came home early one day and discovered the two of them together. It was an awful situation and a terrible decision to have to make - but he decided to forgive her, and start again. Well, the months went by and the two fell back in love and it was is if nothing had ever gone wrong. The husband decided to book them a second honeymoon, so he called up the travel agents, and then phoned his wife to break the good news. When a familiar male voice answered the telephone he feared the worst, went straight home and confronted his wife again. She was alone, there had been no other man she claimed. Nothing was wrong.

In the year that followed she had three affairs, her husband knew of them all, but pretended to be ignorant of them. Eventually she moved out - left a note and disappeared into the early morning with an old case and a mind full of promises from her dozen male friends. They all came to nothing. When her husband finally tracked her down again she was working in a brothel. She was a sick woman, no longer the stunning bride he had married, just a dying prostitute, with no friends or future to look to. It broke his heart to see her wasting away, and though she had hurt him so badly and cost him so much, he could never give up on the one he had always loved. So, with her body no more than a bundle of rags, he lifted her carefully into his arms, paid off the old hag who now owned her and carried her gently home, in the hope that he might bring her back to life and win her love again...

Be careful you don't win the lottery
- only to misplace your ticket.

Life's like a box of chocolates
- you never know what you're gonna get.
Unless of course you take the time to look carefully at the
box and realise that the information is all there for you,
written on the inside of the lid.

Once there was a man and a woman who lived next door to each other. They were both rather shy and so were often unsure what to say to one another. As time went by they began to avoid each other, and became increasingly worried about the possibility of meeting one another. The man began using his back door to come and go, and walked the long way to work to avoid seeing his neighbour in the usual traffic jam. They became so skilled at avoiding one another that soon they weren't sure if they were still neighbours, or indeed if the other person was still living in the same town.

Just to be on the safe side, the man hired a team of labourers to construct a wall between the two premises. However, one day there was a knock on the door, it was the neighbour, her house had been burgled and she needed to use the phone. They chatted for a while, the man helped her clear up, and lent her some of the things she needed. When his car broke down two weeks later she gave him a lift to work. Within six months they had fallen in love, and were wondering why it had taken so long to get to know one another...

A young man marched into a large department store with a shot-gun. When the gun jammed and his plan backfired, the police turned up and, after a struggle, bundled him into the back of their van. However, in their hurry to get back the driver skidded whilst taking a bend, careered over a line of traffic cones and smashed into the back of a patrol car. In the ensuing confusion the young man escaped, with a badly sprained ankle and two black eyes. The following week he returned to the department store and held it up again. This time he was armed with an air pistol which the police tore from his battered fingers as they easily bundled him into the back of their recently repaired van. When the van broke down on the motorway they called out a squad car, but that was called away on route to chase a couple of joyriders. When the breakdown vehicle eventually arrived it was unable to toe the van away as the steering had locked. When the lorry turned up to carry the van away there was no room in the truck for the two policemen and the robber, so the policemen called for another squad car. While they were waiting for this the young man made a break for it, and had to be chased for several hours until he collapsed from exhaustion by the side of the road. Weak and starving he was given shelter by an old widow who lived on the moor. So the police lost all sight of him again.

Three days later he walked into the store again, this time armed with an old crossbow. After a four-hour siege the police finally arrested him and took him to the station where they interrogated him. They discovered his father had originally designed and owned the large department store but in recent years, through crooked deals and aggressive mergers it had been taken from him, inch by inch, floor by floor. All his father had ever wanted was his store back - and his son was willing to risk everything to get it.

When the boy died in custody the story made headline news, and though the new owners of the store never did admit there was any truth in the boy's claims, many of the shareholders then came to visit the old man, to affirm their support, renew old friendships and to offer him their share of the company.

In a legendary country, in a land far away, a man was arrested and charged with living a life of crime. In that country the penalty, should he be found guilty, was death. The night before his trial his closest friend came to visit him and he gave the man some hard advice. Apparently the judge adhered to an unusual code of practice. If a prisoner were to plead guilty then the judge, surprisingly, would declare him innocent. But if the prisoner refused to plead guilty, and claimed innocence, then the judge had no choice but to pronounce him guilty and condemn him to death. The man's friend pleaded with him to admit his guilt, but the risk was a big one. With the death penalty hanging over him, could he have the courage to plead guilty, in the hope of being pronounced innocent?

A man once discovered a suitcase, abandoned in the road. It felt as if it was pretty full but he was too embarrassed to open it in public so he wandered away and left it. A woman came along and did open the case, but she was horrified by the contents and hastily scurried away to tell her friends about it. Before long a man tripped over it and he too had a good look, then went off to write a book on what was inside. Finally a little girl came along, opened the case, saw that it was full, picked it up and carried the whole thing off with her...

A wealthy jeweller had the finest store in town. He'd made millions by living frugally, charging the earth and carefully storing the profit... Until one day a thief broke in, shot him dead and took off with the money. Years later they met again in a rather unpleasant setting. The thief was there for trying to take the old man's money, the jeweller was there for trying to hold on to it...

Faith is like a precious stone. Twist it turn it, examine it and you'll discover many facets. Wear it thoughtfully and humbly and you'll be honoured and recognised. Spend too much time debating its beauty and you'll forget the reason for which you acquired it.

A few months ago I acquired a wonderful new waste bin. I decorated it, polished it and coated it with varnish. I loved this waste bin and carried it everywhere with me, until the day I had a harrowing experience when I brought it out at a party to impress my friends. I proudly passed it round the assembled company and they were all suitably impressed. Then one young man chose to look inside. He reacted immediately and violently to the smell, and then went on to pull out three empty whiskey bottles, a baby's nappy and a dead fish. I don't brag about the bin any more. Although it still shines on the outside.

He is like a huge inflatable ship to jump and play and wrestle and slide on, with walls to leap at and soft corners to press into; marshmallow bannisters for sliding down and doughy nooks to hide in when you want to be alone. And his heart is one huge, billowing banqueting hall with mountains of cushions like barrage balloons for pillow fights and parties. And at night with him you'll never be afraid of the dark, but instead just grow suitably sleepy; except for those glorious, indulgent occasions when you tuck into a midnight feast together. And when the sailing with him finally begins there'll be stories and games and laughter and everyone will be friends. And life will be full of those things which we only dream about now...

The scene is a vast arena. The setting, the end of time. The biggest contest of them all is about to begin. The crowds have gathered in their millions and the stakes are massive. A figure steps onto the stage, an amplified voice announces the team in the blue corner. The lights explode, the music pumps and a stream of gleaming bodies pour like wine across the arena. The red corner follows them and more glittering flesh splashes into view and spills onto the stage. The proud and the strong and the beautiful shimmer like gods under the lights of history. The microphone crackles again, the bell sounds and the display is under way. In the audience the weak and the overlooked stare open-mouthed as the bold and the beautiful display their powers. Suddenly, from nowhere, dark figures explode across the audience, smashing the chairs, tearing the ring apart, hurling bodies to the floor and walls. The very building reels and crumbles under the shock waves, the audience scream and flinch under the flying debris.

A silent horror settles like dust across the auditorium, as the truth begins to dawn - the game is over. Now the contest really begins, and there are no spectators. Audience and competitors alike circle the arena, like sheep they follow one another, shuffling, heads down, while the dark figures crack their whips and choose their victims. At the far end of the room a huge door swings wide and another figure steps in, blinding white and shining like gold. The room freezes and the dark figures recoil in terror. The shining man steps up and talks to each person, it should take a long time but it's all over in the blink of an eye. The dark figures cower in the shadows and are suddenly dispatched, powerless now. The golden figure lifts a case of champagne, rests it on his shoulder and walks into the light leading the crowds down the yellow-lit road. The weaker ones lead the way, the poor, the broken and the children, followed by the others, as the sound of laughter and parties begins to crackle like static across eternity.

On a tube station, late one night, a crowd of people gathered, waiting for the last ride home. As the minutes dragged into hours the people grew restless and began to mutter to one another. Eventually the electronic screen came up with a valid excuse about vandals, leaves, dead animals and broken furniture. Normal service would be resumed. As the faces gawped at this, someone mentioned food. However, even the local McDonalds was shut at that time of night. Other suggestions were proposed and people hunted gloomily in their rucksacks and handbags. Not much was found. One boy produced a full lunch box, but amongst that crowd it wouldn't go far. Someone suggested pooling the little they all had, an old tramp gave advice on scouring the waste bins.

A few teenagers opted to walk half the night to the nearest garage. Others proclaimed the benefits of the chocolate and crisps to be found at an exorbitant price in the station machines. Amongst the clamour for food no one really noticed that most of the kids were busily tucking in to the recently rejected lunch box. The sandwiches were good and fresh and the bottle full of squash seemed to pass round the large group an infinite number of times. Afterwards, while the older children took the leftovers to those out sleeping rough, no one seemed to be able to track down the boy who had first offered his lunch, and the adults wondered why their offspring weren't that interested in the meagre scraps they had managed to scavenge, beg or steal.

Two ex-cons met in a strip-joint. As they chatted they discovered that they had served time in the same prison. Both had been in for armed robbery. "What d'you rob?" asked one. "A liquor store," replied the other, "in Manhattan." He named a street. The other frowned. "You killed my brother," he said. "He ran that place, had a weak heart, the trauma killed him." The other man looked into his drink. "I don't know what to say..." he mumbled. "I never intended that. What about you?" The other man shrugged. "A drugstore, two blocks away." Now the other guy frowned. "That was my brother's store," he said. "He never recovered from the shock." The other man drained his glass. "In that case we're even." he said. "No," said the other, "my brother was 35. That's no age." Another shrug, "Sure, but mine was 18." They faced each other grimly across the table, then turned to watch the oblivious world as it passed them by. Eventually, after an age had passed, they spoke again. "Listen - this isn't easy, but I'm sorry." "Yea, me too." And they each took the other's outstretched hand. "Now we're even," they said.

A young man stands in a market place. His life is for sale. His hands are chained, his body bruised and his head aches from repeated beatings. Three days previously he was abducted, sealed in a sack and transported to this foreign market. Now he is for sale, offered as a prize or a slave - whichever fetches the highest price. He flinches beneath the glare of the sun and the gloating faces, he hasn't eaten since he left home. The outcome is eventually decided, a rich prince will have the boy at a moderate price - he will do for the cleaning, and possibly the cooking too, if he's smart. Before the hammer can connect with the auctioneer's bench a stranger steps into the scene. He raises a hand and immediately doubles the offer. There is a moment of silence, the prince draws breath, then shakes his head. The boy isn't worth the price. The stranger moves up to the platform, he pays the price and loosens the boy's chains. He leads him away from the crowd, hands over a map, money and an air ticket. He tells the boy to go home... The stranger disappears, the boy stumbles into freedom. The ordeal is over.

Walking through town one day I noticed a large silver Rolls Royce. The occupants appeared to be scanning the surrounding shops and buildings. They stopped and asked me the way to a particular building. I described the route as best I could and watched them pull away. When they came to a fork in the road, the right lane looked rather narrow and so, though it took them in the wrong direction, they eased down the left one, I called after them but they had moved out of earshot. I continued walking and took the right fork. A little later they passed me again, just as we were both nearing our destination; however instead of stopping they merely slowed to a crawl, then revved and pulled away again. I continued walking and went inside.

Half an hour later, as I emerged from the building, they were still cruising up and down the road searching for a suitable parking place. For days after that I frequently saw the Rolls Royce as it stalked the roads around that area. But it never found a suitable stopping place, and the occupants never seemed to muster the courage to leave their car, take to their feet, and run towards the place they'd been searching for, for so long...

It was a blustery winter's day when Sam first set up his stall and hardly anyone took any notice. Apart from one old lady and a rather persistent dog who was intent on lubricating Sam's table legs. However, the next day was a Saturday, and a fair one at that, so a good deal more people were in town, and many stopped to read his sign. Some took the bread, some sneered, others were quickly embarrassed. It wasn't until Sunday that he distributed his first glass of wine, and that was also the day the trouble began. A local priest had in fact spotted him on the Saturday and quickly worked out what was going on. When that same man of the cloth found Sam outside again on the Sabbath he had something to say about it. While they argued openly a small crowd gathered to watch, a tramp and two teenagers helped themselves to the wine and the dog returned to sniff the table legs.

A policeman arrived. Then another. And another. Then a traffic warden, two shop owners and a woman priest. By the time the Bishop turned up, Sam had lost his stall, struck a policeman, resisted arrest, and spent a night in a police cell. He awoke with a headache. The Bishop was a thoughtful, understanding fellow. He listened carefully to Sam's account of the story, weighed it up, then replied in careful, measured tones. "You can't just give out communion on the streets, Sam. Not to all and sundry, it's a precious commodity. That's why we have a carefully organised system, a structure in which to prepare the people and the elements so that those who want to receive may do so prayerfully."

Sam shook his head. "And what about those who need to receive it but don't understand church?' he asked. 'What about those who find it boring, or irrelevant, but still want to reach out and find some kind of hope?"

The Bishop nodded.

"I know what you're saying Sam,' he said, 'and that's why we must find ways to make our faith more accessible to those outside the church." Sam grabbed at the other man's coat. "That's what I was trying to do!" he yelled, then sobering up again he continued, "Not long ago I sat in a church service when a tramp wandered in and sat beside me. It was during the Bible reading so, being a coward, I thought it inappropriate to speak to him at that point. The sermon followed immediately after, so that was difficult too. A few minutes later he got up and left. I followed him after that - but he'd gone. There was nothing there to touch his world, yet when Jesus first gave bread and wine it was in the context of a simple, commonly-shared meal! What a gift, we all love eating..."

The Bishop nodded, stood up and left. The following week Sam had left that place and moved on to hand out bread and wine in the next town.

23083454R00088

Printed in Great Britain
by Amazon